Alexis de Tocqueville

Series Introduction

The *Major Conservative and Libertarian Thinkers* series aims to show that there is a rigorous, scholarly tradition of social and political thought that may be broadly described as 'conservative', 'libertarian' or some combination of the two.

The series aims to show that conservatism is not simply a reaction against contemporary events, nor a privileging of intuitive thought over deductive reasoning; libertarianism is not simply an apology for unfettered capitalism or an attempt to justify a misguided atomistic concept of the individual. Rather, the thinkers in this series have developed coherent intellectual positions that are grounded in empirical reality and also founded upon serious philosophical reflection on the relationship between the individual and society, how the social institutions necessary for a free society are to be established and maintained, and the implications of the limits to human knowledge and certainty.

Each volume in the series presents a thinker's ideas in an accessible and cogent manner to provide an indispensable work for both students with varying degrees of familiarity with the topic as well as more advanced scholars.

The following twenty volumes that make up the entire *Major Conservative and Libertarian Thinkers* series are written by international scholars and experts.

The Salamanca School by Andre Azevedo Alves (LSE, UK) &
 Professor José Manuel Moreira (Porto, Portugal)
Thomas Hobbes by Dr R. E. R. Bunce (Cambridge, UK)
John Locke by Professor Eric Mack (Tulane, US)
David Hume by Professor Christopher J. Berry (Glasgow, UK)
Adam Smith by Professor James Otteson (Yeshiva, US)
Edmund Burke by Professor Dennis O'Keeffe (Buckingham, UK)
Alexis de Tocqueville by Dr Alan S Kahan (Paris, France)
Herbert Spencer by Alberto Mingardi (Istituto Bruno Leoni, Italy)
Ludwig von Mises by Richard Ebeling (Trinity College)

Joseph A. Schumpeter by Professor John Medearis (Riverside, California, US)
F. A. Hayek by Dr Adam Tebble (UCL, UK)
Michael Oakeshott by Dr Edmund Neill (Oxford, UK)
Karl Popper by Dr Phil Parvin (Cambridge, UK)
Ayn Rand by Professor Mimi Gladstein (Texas, US)
Milton Friedman by Dr William Ruger (Texas State, US)
James M. Buchanan by Dr John Meadowcroft (King's College London, UK)
The Modern Papacy by Dr Samuel Gregg (Acton Institute, US)
Robert Nozick by Ralf Bader (St Andrews, UK)
Russell Kirk by Jon Pafford
Murray Rothbard by Gerard Casey

Of course, in any series of this nature, choices have to be made as to which thinkers to include and which to leave out. Two of the thinkers in the series – F. A. Hayek and James M. Buchanan – have written explicit statements rejecting the label 'conservative'. Similarly, other thinkers, such as David Hume and Karl Popper, may be more accurately described as classical liberals than either conservatives or libertarians. But these thinkers have been included because a full appreciation of this particular tradition of thought would be impossible without their inclusion; conservative and libertarian thought cannot be fully understood without some knowledge of the intellectual contributions of Hume, Hayek, Popper and Buchanan, among others. While no list of conservative and libertarian thinkers can be perfect, then, it is hoped that the volumes in this series come as close as possible to providing a comprehensive account of the key contributors to this particular tradition.

John Meadowcroft
King's College London

Alexis de Tocqueville

Alan S. Kahan

Major Conservative and
Libertarian Thinkers

Series Editor: John Meadowcroft

Volume 7

BLOOMSBURY

NEW YORK • LONDON • NEW DELHI • SYDNEY

Bloomsbury Academic
An imprint of Bloomsbury Publishing Plc

175 Fifth Avenue   50 Bedford Square
New York   London
NY 10010   WC1B 3DP
USA   UK

www.bloomsbury.com

Hardback edition first published in 2010 by the Continuum International
Publishing Group Inc

This paperback edition publish by Bloomsbury Academic 2013

© Alan S. Kahan, 2013

Library of Congress Cataloging-in-Publication Data
A catalog record for this book is available from the Library of Congress.

ISBN: HB: 978-0-8264-8313-3
PB: 978-1-4411-7327-0

Typeset by Deanta Global Publishing Services, Chennai, India
Printed and bound in the United States of America

Contents

Series Editor's Preface

Alexis de Tocqueville was the author of two masterpieces, *Democracy in America*, his best-known work today, and *The Old Regime and the Revolution*. In these two works Tocqueville addressed the prospects for freedom in the transition from aristocratic regimes to democratic societies. Tocqueville believed that democracy could promise new vistas of freedom; more and more people could enjoy "the pleasure of being able to speak, act, and breathe without constraint." But he also foresaw that democracy could pose an enormous new threat to freedom; the tyranny of the majority could create a culture of stultifying conformity in which the scope for individual autonomy was severely limited. As such, Tocqueville captured the essential ambiguity towards democracy that is characteristic of libertarian and conservative thought; democracy is perceived to have the power to both emancipate and enslave, so the spread of democracy need not necessarily be synonymous with the advance of freedom.

In this outstanding book Dr Alan S. Kahan, one of the world's leading authorities on Tocqueville's work, presents an accessible and rigorous account of Tocqueville's ideas set in the context of the Frenchman's life and times. The book provides a vivid account of Tocqueville's life and goes on to set out the essential tensions and ambiguities in Tocqueville's thought and analyze the ideas that make him such a compelling and insightful thinker. Kahan then charts the response to Tocqueville's work by his contemporaries, before showing the enduring relevance of Tocqueville's intellectual contribution.

In so doing, this volume makes a crucial contribution to the *Major Conservative and Libertarian Thinkers* series. This exceptional book will prove indispensable to those unfamiliar with Tocqueville's work as well as to more advanced scholars in the history of ideas and democratic theory.

John Meadowcroft
King's College London

Part I

1

Biography

Alexis de Tocqueville, who understood democracy better than anyone else ever did, was born into one of France's oldest aristocratic families on July 29, 1805. But he was not born in a castle. He was born in a rented Paris apartment. The world he was born into was not the one in which his family had been bred. It was a new world, a revolutionary world, a world in which an aristocrat was always something of an outsider. It was characteristic of Tocqueville's life that he was always both an insider and an outsider.

Tocqueville was a member of the old elite, and for that reason an outsider in the new France, the France born in the French Revolution of 1789. Throughout his life he had to struggle for acceptance by those distrustful of his aristocratic origins. He firmly believed in the superiority of the new democratic society, yet he was socially uncomfortable with people who did not come from his own caste. Despite this discomfort, he broke tradition by marrying a woman who was not only not a French aristocrat, but English, middle class and six years his elder. For the rest of his life he engaged in a hopeless struggle to make his family accept her. Breaking politically with his father and brothers, he accepted the revolution of 1830 that expelled the restored Bourbon monarchy, and he swore an oath of allegiance to the new king, Louis-Philippe, the Duke of Orleans. Distrusted by both his Legitimist family and friends (Legitimists were those who supported the Bourbon dynasty, the "legitimate" rulers) and his new Orleanist allies, he sailed off to America – where he was once again an outsider. When he was elected to the National Assembly he joined the opposition, which was reluctant to accept him. Throughout his career, as both a writer and a politician, Tocqueville always felt isolated. He thought he was really understood only by a handful, and even then not completely. Perhaps it was his dual perspective as both insider and outsider that allowed him to see democracy so clearly.

Tocqueville's aristocratic roots went deep. Very few noble families in France could trace their ancestors as far back as he could. One of them helped William the Conqueror invade England in 1066. Since the seventeenth century, at least, the family had been large landowners in western Normandy. They owned several estates not far from the English Channel, one of which was near the village of Tocqueville, from which they took their name. While the Tocquevilles were an old family, they were not an illustrious one (although Marshal Vauban was an ancestor on the paternal side). However, Alexis' parents were something of an exception. His father, Hervé de Tocqueville, served the restored Bourbon monarchy as an administrator after 1815. He was eventually named to the Chamber of Peers, the upper house of the French legislature under the restored Bourbon monarchy, and granted a peerage and the formal title of Comte (count) de Tocqueville. In retirement he wrote a history of the French Revolution.

Hervé was nineteen when the French Revolution broke out in 1789. He married Alexis' mother, Louise de Rosanbo, four years later, in early 1793. Her family was both wealthy and distinguished. She came from a different sort of nobility than the Tocquevilles. The Tocquevilles were members of the *noblesse d'épée*, the "sword nobility," families who had attained their status through military service to the king. The Rosanbos were members of the *noblesse de robe*, the "robe nobility," who had been ennobled for their service as judges and administrators. Louise de Rosanbo was the granddaughter of the great Malesherbes, a judge, a noted opponent of royal authority in the decades before the Revolution and an intellectual figure of the French Enlightenment.

Louise de Rosanbo's elder sister had married the brother of the great French Romantic writer Chateaubriand, who was thus a cousin to Alexis. Through this marriage Alexis was connected by blood to leading figures in French intellectual life.

Louise was pretty, and came from a wealthy family. She was also mentally unstable, subject to nervous fits and extended bouts of depression; Alexis too was subject to depression to some extent. Her mental condition was not improved by the events that succeeded her marriage. Although an enemy of royal absolutism, Malesherbes was a supporter of the monarchy. When the king was put on trial Malesherbes acted as lawyer for the defense. As a result, in December 1793, Malesherbes and the rest of the family, including Hervé and Louise, were arrested. Malesherbes and several other family members were guillotined the following April. Hervé's hair turned white in prison. It was just a matter of time before he and his wife would die too. They were scheduled for trial and execution on July 30, but on July 27 Robespierre's radical government was overthrown, and in October they were set free. Had Robespierre's fall come a few days later, Alexis de Tocqueville would never have been born.

He was the middle child of three brothers. Like them, the young Alexis was at first tutored at home by a Catholic priest of Jansenist tendencies, the abbé Le Sueur (Jansenism was a seventeenth-century Catholic movement with which Pascal, an important influence on Tocqueville, was associated). The abbé recognized his unusual abilities. When it was suggested that Alexis be destined for a military career, he responded that it would be a waste to hide such great talent under a helmet. Later, Alexis was sent to high school in Metz, where his father was serving the restored monarchy as prefect (chief administrative officer of the department). Alexis had a good deal of free time there, some of which he spent in his father's very considerable library (he was also wounded in a duel, and had his first love affairs). Although his mother was very devout, his father was no more religious than appearances required. His library contained many eighteenth-century Enlightenment authors who rejected

Christianity. In reading them, the young Alexis lost his Catholic faith at the age of sixteen, although he remained profoundly concerned with religious questions all his life. It was likely also in this library that Tocqueville made the acquaintance for the first time of those he would describe as the "three authors he carried with him everywhere," Pascal, Montesquieu and Rousseau (*OC,* 1977a, 418). Their influence on his thought was profound.

After he finished high school, Tocqueville went to Paris to study law. His father had felt embarrassed by his lack of legal knowledge when he first went into administration. Law was also the traditional career of his mother's family. It was certainly appropriate training for someone contemplating a career in administration or politics or both, the kind of career for which Alexis seemed destined. The concern for legal questions and legal systems Tocqueville shows throughout his writing owes much to his initial training, often overlooked by commentators.

Tocqueville studied law for two years, graduating in 1826. He was then appointed an assistant public prosecutor at Versailles, serving effectively as an unpaid trainee. But Tocqueville did not merely continue his legal training at Versailles. It was at Versailles that both his personal and his intellectual life took on their mature shape. He became friends with his new, slightly senior colleague Gustave de Beaumont, another young noble from a royalist family. Tocqueville had the good fortune of being able to maintain several lifelong friendships, but of all these, the friendship with Beaumont was probably the most important. Beaumont would be his companion on his voyage to America and the first editor of his collected works. Their collected correspondence fills three volumes. At Versailles, Tocqueville also met the woman he was to marry, Mary Mottley, who lived nearby caring for an elderly aunt.

Tocqueville's Versailles period was also fertile in intellectual influences. He began to study modern history (in high school he had studied the Greeks and Romans). He seems to have begun his serious reading with the work of an historian and politician he would later despise, the ten-volume History of the French Revolution by Adolphe Thiers. After the royalist piety in which he was raised, it came as a revelation to him. Still more of a revelation were the lectures on French history he attended given by the historian, political theorist and later prime minister of France François Guizot. That Tocqueville was later Guizot's political opponent must not be allowed to obscure the fact that Guizot was a great influence on him. Guizot was a masterful lecturer, and Tocqueville and Beaumont regularly attended his lectures, taking copious notes, which they shared with one another. What struck them were less the particulars of Guizot's arguments than the broad historical and sociological sweep he brought to bear on his analysis of French history. Guizot's methods would later influence much of Tocqueville's writing.

In 1830, revolution broke out once again in France. Tocqueville sympathized with the revolutionaries' cause, while retaining a deep emotional attachment to the ruling Bourbon dynasty. As so often, he felt both an insider and an outsider. In some torment, he took the oath of loyalty to the new regime of King Louis-Philippe that was demanded of all public officials who wanted to retain their positions. His father and brothers refused. Caught in this difficult position, and with a cloudy future facing him as a lawyer for the new government with family ties to the old regime, Tocqueville decided it would be best to leave France for a while. Together with Beaumont, he petitioned for a leave of absence to study one of the trendy subjects of the day, prison reform, in the country that was widely considered to be the leading pioneer in the field, America. On March 29, 1831, they took ship for New York. Tocqueville would remain in the United States until February 20, 1832. But prison reform was not the chief thing on the travelers' minds. In America, they would see democracy in action. In America, they would see the future of France. From the moment he set foot on the boat, Tocqueville was thinking about democracy.

Tocqueville's (and Beaumont's) nearly year-long journey through America has been the subject of many books and not a few repetitions by later writers. He saw much of what was then the United States (and a little of Canada), but not all of it. The bulk of his time was spent in the cities of the northeast; Boston New York and Philadelphia; in Baltimore (which at the time was culturally in the Upper South); in the then wilderness of Michigan; and in the frontier territory along the Ohio and Mississippi rivers in the states of Ohio, Kentucky and Tennessee. He took a steamboat down the Mississippi to New Orleans, and he was intending to spend a few months in the southeast United States when he was recalled home by the government. A quick journey mostly by coach from New Orleans to Washington, where Tocqueville shook President Jackson's hand and was unimpressed, and a return via Baltimore to New York, put Tocqueville on a ship back to France.

In America, Tocqueville talked to everyone he could, and as a wealthy young French aristocrat who spoke English, he could talk to almost anyone he wanted, from a former president such as John Quincy Adams to Michigan Indian chiefs who remembered French Canada with fondness. He has been criticized for not spending time in the South, and for speaking mostly to supporters of the defeated Federalist Party rather than with Jacksonian democrats, but to a certain extent such criticisms are misguided. Although Tocqueville himself said that he had only acquired a "superficial" knowledge of the South, and regretted not being able to spend another six months there as planned, Tocqueville *did* talk with many Southerners, if not with many people from South Carolina (*OC*, 1998b, 165). Maryland was a southern, slave-holding state, and Tocqueville recorded significant conversations and experiences there. On the steamboat down the Mississippi, Tocqueville recorded a long and important conversation with Sam Houston, after whom the Texas city of Houston is named. He spent three days in New Orleans, and elsewhere recorded extended conversations with Southerners he met. If he did not spend as much time in the deep South as he would have wished, he certainly talked about it with men who knew it well, both Southerners and Northerners. It is true he did not talk with many Jacksonians, but it seems unlikely that such conversations would have changed his attitudes.

When Tocqueville and Beaumont returned to France, their first task was to write the report on the American penitentiary system they had officially been sent to prepare. This was almost entirely written by Beaumont, but published under both names in 1832. It was a modest success. Tocqueville soon turned to other projects. He visited England in 1833, and he returned there and visited Ireland in 1835. He became acquainted with the English philosopher John Stuart Mill, who would in due course write brilliant reviews of Tocqueville's work on America. But Tocqueville's objective was not merely to travel. His immediate goals were twofold: overcoming the objections of his family to marrying Mary Mottley, which came to pass in 1835, and writing the first volume of *Democracy in America*, which was published the same year.

Tocqueville's marriage to Mary Mottley, like his oath of allegiance to the new regime, was a public act of nonconformity of the sort he usually went to some lengths to avoid. However much he was an outsider in his thoughts and feelings, he always took pains to conform to social expectations. For example, he could not take communion in good conscience, but he could and did regularly attend church, and otherwise act in the ways considered appropriate for a man of his class. His marriage was the sole ongoing exception to the rule. Mary, or Marie as she became known, was by birth an English Protestant. That she converted to Catholicism before marrying Alexis, or that she became by far the more devout of the two, could not change her outsider status. Much would have been forgiven her had she been wealthy, but while no pauper, her wealth was certainly much less than Alexis' own. The fact that she was six years older than Tocqueville was also unconventional. Stormy as their relationship was at times (Marie was jealous, often with justification), it was also marked by a lasting passion and affection that was unconventional in aristocratic marriages of the period.

Democracy in America was not a conventional book either. Masterpieces rarely are. However, it was a great success in conventional terms. It received enthusiastic reviews, to which a well-thought out publicity campaign by Tocqueville contributed. He took care to send copies to all the right people, several of whom were more or less distant cousins. The book was widely noticed, in England and America as well as in France. Tocqueville soon became one of the stars of the Paris literary scene, welcomed at all the best salons. After 1835, Tocqueville was famous.

But he was not content with his literary and intellectual reputation. He wanted more. Tocqueville's character was always characterized by a mixture of depression, stoicism and vaulting ambition, as can be seen in this 1835 letter to a friend. "The older I get, the more I see life from the perspective I thought was due to the enthusiasm of my first youth. A thing of mediocre value, which is only worthwhile to the extent that one uses it to do one's duty, help people, and take one's rank among them." Tocqueville was anxious to make his way to the front rank on the political stage, too. In 1837, when he was making his first efforts towards a political career, he wrote again: "Don't think, my dear friend, that I have an unthinking enthusiasm or even any enthusiasm at all for the intellectual life. I have always put action above everything else" (*OC*, 1977a, 376, 479). Tocqueville intended to use his new-found reputation as a great writer and political thinker to become a political leader. After some hesitation, he chose to run for election from a district in Normandy, in which the chateau of Tocqueville, which he had recently inherited on his mother's death, was located. The prime minister at the time was another one of Tocqueville's cousins, Count Molé. He offered to support Tocqueville's candidacy, which would surely have guaranteed Tocqueville's victory. But Alexis refused, insisting that to do otherwise would mean sacrificing his political independence. Refusing the benefits of his insider position, he preferred to remain an outsider. He wished to be independent of any political party, not a public and committed supporter of the conservative government. He lost, narrowly, by a vote of

247 to 210.[1] In 1839 he ran again, and this time he was elected. He would represent the same district in the French parliament for the next thirteen years, until Napoleon III's coup d'état drove him out of politics.

Tocqueville's entry into politics did not prevent him from finishing *Democracy in America*, whose second and final volume was published in 1840. Much to his chagrin, it did not receive quite the same warm welcome as volume one. More abstract and theoretical, many readers found it hard to follow. The reviews were correspondingly less enthusiastic, and sales slower. Nevertheless, it served to cement Tocqueville's literary reputation.

However much he wanted to be independent, Tocqueville did not wish to remain on the fringes of parliamentary life. As he wrote to Pierre-Paul Royer-Collard, an elderly liberal writer and former politician who became something of a father-figure to Tocqueville at this time (his own father being politically far removed from Alexis' views, however much the two remained affectionate towards one another), "my nature is to be active and, I must admit, ambitious. I would like power, if it could be honorably acquired and kept." The problem was that Tocqueville was not comfortable with any of the existing political parties. He wanted in, but found that character, temperament and political perspective forced him to remain an outsider. He was a liberal, as that word was used in nineteenth-century France, but as he described himself, a "liberal of a new kind," one whose love of freedom was coupled with respect for existing institutions and for religion. As he wrote in a note to himself, "I have an intellectual preference for democratic institutions, but I am aristocratic by instinct, that is I despise and fear the crowd. I passionately love freedom, legality, the respect for rights, but not democracy. This is the base of my soul." Views like these made it hard for Tocqueville to commit himself wholeheartedly to any

---

[1] Under the July Monarchy (1830–1848), only the wealthiest 2–3% of French adult males could vote.

political party, or to attract others' support for his own. Ambivalence is rarely a crowd-pleaser (*Reader*, 2002, 153, 160, 219).

Tocqueville was handicapped in his political career in other ways as well. In nineteenth-century politics the ability to speak well and at length was a necessity for anyone with political ambition. Tocqueville was a capable speaker, but he found it increasingly difficult to speak for long periods of time. From the late 1830s he was intermittently in poor physical health, perhaps already showing signs of the tuberculosis that would kill him. In addition, temperamentally he found it hard to suffer fools, and he was never adept, to say the least, at collegial backslapping and moral flexibility. When he attempted to form his own parliamentary block, he found he could attract only a handful or two of supporters. He remained a political "name," someone who would be listened to when he spoke from the rostrum, but he was never a political power, not as long as the July Monarchy lasted, that is, until the Revolution of 1848.

He continued to try, however. All the major political groups controlled newspapers, so Tocqueville bought his own, *Le Commerce*, which he owned and operated in 1844–45. He quickly got caught in the middle of a fight over Catholic private schools. The Left wanted to refuse them recognition, the Right wanted them funded by the state. Tocqueville's middle ground, supporting their right to recognition but rejecting their right to state funding, made him popular with nobody. The newspaper lost circulation rapidly, and Tocqueville sold it. He was no more successful in his other attempts to influence public policy. He tried to persuade France to abolish slavery, but his bills to do so were never adopted. He attempted to foster decentralization, but found little sympathy for his cause. He was somewhat more successful in influencing government policy in the new French colony of Algeria, which he visited in 1841 and 1846, but not very much. He was increasingly frustrated by what he saw as the petty personal politics of the July Monarchy, in which both the government and the opposition were, in his view, unprincipled men motivated by selfish interests. In 1847 he tried to form a new political party, the "Young Left," but could barely attract two dozen deputies to his side. He was afraid that France was as frustrated with such a government as he was, and that the result would be a revolution he did not want. In the only famous speech of his July Monarchy political career, given on January 29, 1848, just a few weeks before the revolution, he warned the government and the rest of the politicians that they were sleeping atop a volcano. He urged them to stop their petty bickering and address the nation's real needs: those of the working classes who were increasingly turning to socialist ideas. Everything appeared calm, but, he warned the deputies "have you no intuitive instinct . . . that tells you the ground is trembling once more in Europe? Do you not feel – how shall I say it – a revolutionary wind in the air?" (*Reader*, 2002, 237). They did not. Neither, Tocqueville admitted in his posthumously published *Recollections* of 1848, did he, really. But he was right. Oddly enough, it was the Revolution of 1848 that would bring Tocqueville the most political power and influence he would ever enjoy.

On February 22 the revolution began, and by the February 24 King Louis-Philippe had abdicated and the Republic had been proclaimed. Tocqueville took advantage of the circumstances to write a new preface to *Democracy in America*, suggesting that the February revolution was further evidence that he was right that democracy was inevitable. The first cheap edition of the *Democracy* was produced, and sold out its four thousand copies. Two more editions were brought out and sold. Elections were called for a new Constituent Assembly, elections that would for the first time in French history be based on universal manhood suffrage. Tocqueville's electorate would now number in the hundreds of thousands, instead of a few hundreds.

Tocqueville left Paris to return to Normandy to campaign. His campaign platform rejected the monarchy and socialism with equal firmness. This was just what rural France (despite the presence of the channel port of Cherbourg in his redrawn district, most of it was rural) was looking for. Election day, April 23, 1848, was one of the great triumphs of Tocqueville's life. His *Recollections* tells the story. On that day, the voters of the little village of Tocqueville assembled to walk together to the polling place, some five kilometers (three miles) away. They lined up in alphabetical order. Tocqueville took his place among the Ts, "for I knew that in democratic times and countries one must allow oneself to be put at the head of the people, but must not put oneself there" (*Recollections*, 1987, 95). Shortly before they arrived at the poll, the group stopped and insisted that Tocqueville make them a speech. He did, urging them to give serious consideration to the importance of what they were doing. He got a round of applause, and nearly unanimous support at the ballot box. He ended up with over 110,000 votes out of a possible total of about 120,000. For once, his aristocratic feudal self could take equal satisfaction with his democratic side. But Tocqueville remained a divided soul. His personal satisfaction was diminished by his dislike for the revolutionary circumstances in which it had come. From the moment the February Revolution took place, Tocqueville feared that France was headed for a future that would alternate between anarchy and despotism, and events were to prove him not far wrong.

Tocqueville, as the great expert on America, the great republic, was naturally named to the committee that was to draft the constitution for the new French republic. Unfortunately, he soon discovered that he was once more an outsider, condemned to take a secondary role. There was little support on the committee for decentralizing French government and giving more power to local governments or private associations. His proposal to create a two-chamber legislature was quickly dismissed. Where he was among the majority, as, for example, in making the president ineligible for reelection, he later regretted his position.

When in mid-June the constitution was finished, consideration of it was postponed while another attempt at revolution was defeated. The workers of Paris had risen again, this time to demand a more socially radical regime. This time, unlike in February, the government fought back, not just with the support of the army but with that of the middle classes and the provinces, which volunteered *en masse* to fight against the revolution in Paris. In four days of fighting, the "June Days," the revolution was crushed, at the cost of perhaps five thousand lives. Tocqueville was pleased at the result. He had some sympathy for the poor, but none for socialism. When the new constitution was debated, he gave a speech against the socialist idea of including a "right to work" in the document.

However, if Tocqueville was pleased with the suppression of the June revolt, he was not pleased with the state of France. Even if he was exhilarated by the end of the petty politics of the July Monarchy, he was depressed when he considered France's future. Through the end of his life, his letters about French politics are filled with pessimistic remarks about the long-term future of France. As he wrote to a friend in July of 1848:

> I do not have faith in the future. I feel a profound sadness that rises much less from immediate apprehensions (although they are great) than from the absence of hope. I do not know if I should still hope to see established in our country a government that is at the same time regular, strong, and liberal. This ideal was the dream of my entire youth, as you know . . . Is it permissible to still believe in its realization? . . . Are we not on a stormy sea without a shore? . . . It is not only such a government that seems impossible, but any durable government whatsoever, and that we are destined to oscillate for a long time between despotism and liberty, without being able to permanently support either? (*SL*, 1985, 215)

The new constitution was adopted. Tocqueville was elected to the new National Assembly, and Louis-Napoleon Bonaparte, to the surprise of everyone except himself, was elected by the French nation as its first president. Tocqueville was reelected, and shortly thereafter, for the first and last time in his life, held national office, as foreign minister in the new government formed by prime minister Odilon Barrot.

Tocqueville's time as foreign minister was brief, only five months (June–October 1849) before the Barrot government fell. He chiefly had to defend a foreign policy he had not made and did not entirely approve of, that is, French military intervention in Italy to restore Rome to the control of the Pope. Fundamentally, he recognized both France's relative weakness and its need to appear strong, and he was a keen observer of the ongoing turmoil in Germany, struggling with its own revolutions and tormented by various attempts to unite the many German states into a single country. He maintained, for the rest of his life, a close watch on the German scene. Tocqueville recognized that Germany, if united, was a potential great power. He feared that the Napoleonic Wars had made Germans so hostile to France that they would fail to recognize the common threat posed to both countries by a power Tocqueville feared far more: Russia. A few years later, during of the Crimean War, which pitted England, France and Turkey against the czar, Tocqueville would foresee much of the future history of the West's relationship with Russia:

> I think . . . that Russia is a great danger to Europe . . . But I am deeply convinced that it is not by taking from her a town, or even a province, nor by diplomatic precautions, still less by placing sentinels along her frontier, that the Western Powers will permanently stop her progress.
>
> A temporary bulwark may be raised against her, but a mere accident may destroy it, or a change of alliances or a domestic policy may render it useless.
>
> I am convinced that Russia can be stopped only by raising before her powers created by the hatred which she inspires, whose vital and constant interest it shall be to keep themselves united and to keep her in. In other words, by the resurrection of Poland, and by the re-animation of Turkey.
>
> I do not believe that either of these means can now be adopted. The detestable jealousies and ambitions of the European nations resemble, as you say in your letter, nothing

better than the quarrels of the Greeks in the face of Philip. Not one will sacrifice her passions or her objects. (*Correspondence with Senior*, 2004b, September 19, 1855)

But Tocqueville was in no position to implement grand strategy. His diplomacy scored some humanitarian victories protecting political refugees, but on the whole Tocqueville as foreign minister played with a weak hand and correspondingly had unremarkable success.

After the Barrot government fell Tocqueville, now clearly suffering from tuberculosis, asked for a leave of absence from the Assembly on grounds of ill-health. In July of 1850 he went to Italy to recuperate from a severe attack. At Sorrento, near Naples, he wrote his *Recollections* of the events of 1848, intended for posthumous publication, and there he conceived the project of writing a history of the French Revolution.

When he returned to France in April of 1851 the country was clearly in political crisis. Louis-Napoleon was highly popular in the country and highly unwilling to leave power. The problem was that his reelection as president was unconstitutional, thanks to the constitution Tocqueville had helped write. Unlike many of his fellow politicians, Tocqueville did not hold Louis-Napoleon in contempt, and he was prepared to cooperate with him provided he could be kept in constitutional bounds. When it became clear that the president would be difficult to dislodge from power, Tocqueville fought to amend the constitution to permit the reelection of the president. Unfortunately, the constitution provided for a near-impossible amendment process, and the effort failed.

On December 2, 1851, Louis-Napoleon launched the coup d'état that would make him Emperor Napoleon III. Tocqueville was arrested along with some two hundred other members of the Assembly, and spent a few days in prison with them. Napoleon III, in a gesture of personal respect for Tocqueville, offered to let him out early, but Tocqueville refused (another example of Tocqueville preferring to remain an outsider).

Tocqueville smuggled out to England a letter denouncing the coup, which was published in the *London Times*, on December 11. Rather than take a loyalty oath to the new government, Tocqueville resigned his position as president of his departmental council. Although later Napoleon III would sound him out about returning as foreign minister, and never ceased to testify his personal regard for Tocqueville, Tocqueville remained a resolute opponent of the Second Empire, as the new regime was called, until his death.

As an opponent of the Empire, political life was closed to Tocqueville. He grew furious with his brothers when they gave their support to the new regime. With political action closed to him, he returned to political thought. The project he had conceived in Sorrento for writing a history of the French Revolution became his full-time occupation. Originally Tocqueville had planned to focus on Napoleon, but as time went on his focus shifted to the "old regime," the decades and even centuries that led up to the Revolution of 1789 itself. The details of that work will be discussed later. Its immediate impact on Tocqueville's life was to make him a pilgrim of the archives. He spent a winter working in the archives at Tours, and he used his privileges as a former member of the Assembly to borrow books from the national library in Paris and take them to Tocqueville when he could not work in Paris.

Tocqueville did not restrict his travel to libraries, however. In the interest of comparing France to other European nations, he taught himself German, and in 1854 set off on a tour of Germany, intending to travel as far as Berlin (he also contemplated a trip to Russia). But Marie, who accompanied him, soon suffered physical problems and the trip had to be cut short after a visit to the Rhine region in western Germany. They returned to France and he wrote, in fits and starts. In June of 1856 *The Old Regime and the Revolution* was published, intended to be the first volume of a two-volume history of the Revolution.

Once again, Tocqueville was a great success as an author. Although there were some hostile reviews by those whose political views the book offended, it was generally regarded as another masterpiece. This grand reception for a work that clearly rejected political tyranny and, by implication, the Second Empire ought to have mitigated Tocqueville's pessimism about his country's future, but it did not, at least in the short run. As he wrote Odilon Barrot, "It is still useful to throw these ideas into circulation in the hope that, if they are correct, they will end up little by little transforming themselves into passions and into facts. I ask God to let me see that transformation in my days, although, to tell the truth, I hardly hope so" (Kahan 2001, 132).

The publication of *The Old Regime* also led to a renewed correspondence between Tocqueville and J. S. Mill, whose praise thrilled Tocqueville. It also occasioned a brief but significant correspondence with Arthur de Gobineau. Gobineau had served as Tocqueville's secretary when he was minister of foreign affairs. Today he is known as the leading nineteenth-century exponent of "scientific" racism. Tocqueville took the opportunity to reject Gobineau's views in the strongest possible terms.

In 1857 Tocqueville once again visited England. He wanted to work on the collections of French Revolutionary documents in the British Museum, and on other documents in the British Foreign Office archives. He was the social lion of the season, partly because of his book, partly because of his principled opposition to Napoleon III. Now, too, he was an ex-minister and after the reception his book had received, he was considered an even more prominent leader of the liberal opposition to Napoleon III. To those who mattered in England, it was evident that Tocqueville was a person who had once mattered in France's political life and might matter again. He spent an hour with Prince Albert, the royal consort, and had to turn down an invitation to dinner from Lord Palmerston, the prime minister. On his return Tocqueville was transported back to Normandy aboard a British naval vessel, something that very much impressed his neighbors and Napoleon's political police, who forbade public mention of it.

Despite his English research, Tocqueville only made slow progress on volume two of *The Old Regime*. Tocqueville had always been anxious about his writing, which tended to happen in bursts. His inability to complete the second volume has given rise to numerous explanations by commentators. Most likely, however, the explanation is prosaic, and medical: Tocqueville was dying, although he didn't know it. He was increasingly ill with what would become his final attack of tuberculosis. By the fall of 1858, his doctors told him that he could not spend another winter at Tocqueville, and sent him to Cannes, on the Mediterranean coast in the south of France. After a winter of terrible suffering, Alexis de Tocqueville died on April 16, 1859.

One aspect of his death resulted in some controversy. Marie, who had become an ardent Catholic, made great efforts to insure a deathbed conversion by Tocqueville, who resisted them. The question is whether she succeeded in the end. There is considerable information about Tocqueville's personal views on religion in his last years, from his correspondence with Madame de Swetchine, a Russian aristocrat living in Paris who had converted to Catholicism. In that correspondence it is clear that Tocqueville, rather to his own regret, maintained the more or less Deist views he had adopted as a teenager. As an adult he did not take communion. However, a few days before his death, he heard mass, confessed and received communion. Had the outsider decided to become an insider? Whether this was merely a parting gift to his wife will never be known.

Part II

2

The Essential Tocqueville

When reading Tocqueville, it is easy to be captured by the fluid style, the brilliant phrases, the subject he is discussing. But it is essential never to lose sight of his central concerns. Whether he is writing about the American judicial system, the colonization of Algeria or French municipal administration under Louis XIV, Tocqueville is guided by the same values, uses the same methods, betrays the same influences and has the same goals in mind. Superficially, his work may be a study in contrasts. There does not seem to be much in common in the subjects of his two masterpieces, *Democracy in America* and *The Old Regime and the Revolution*. Indeed, much scholarly ink has been spilled over whether the second volume of *Democracy in America* does not contradict some of the conclusions of the first, or whether the projected second volume of *The Old Regime* might not have done the same with regard to the French Revolution. Nonetheless, Tocqueville is one of the most consistent political theorists ever to write more than one book. What is essential in Tocqueville are two moral commitments, a commitment to freedom and a commitment to France.

The moral foundation of Tocqueville's work was a commitment to freedom. Both *Democracy in America* and *The Old Regime* are essentially about freedom. As he wrote in a note to himself, "Freedom is the first of my passions. This is what is true." Tocqueville's life work was an effort to discover how freedom could be preserved, created or extended in the democratic societies of the modern world. In writing about democracy in America,

"My purpose was to show, by using America as an example, that laws and above all mores could allow a democratic people to remain free" (*Reader*, 2002, 220; *Democracy*, 2004, 364).

People understand "freedom" in many different ways. A full consideration of "Tocqueville's Concept of Freedom" would require a volume in itself, but a few words about it are necessary here. Tocqueville's own definition of freedom is "the pleasure of being able to speak, act, and breathe without constraint, under the government of God and the laws alone." Tocqueville was always devoted to freedom, and loved it instinctively. He did not want to give a reason for why freedom deserved to be loved: "that which, in all times, has so strongly attached certain men's hearts to freedom, are its own attractions, its own peculiar charm, independent of its benefits . . . Whoever seeks for anything from freedom but itself is made for slavery . . . One must give up on making this comprehensible to the mediocre souls who have never felt it." Tocqueville's thirst for freedom was intensely personal (*Reader*, 2004, 153; *OR*, 1998a, 217).

Tocqueville's attachment to freedom was not just a caprice, however. For Tocqueville, freedom is the basis of all human achievement. "All my reflections lead me to believe that no moral and political greatness is possible for long without [freedom]. I am therefore as strongly attached to freedom as to morality . . ." For Tocqueville, freedom is the source of great human actions and great human beings, indeed of almost everything worth having: "That nothing is more prodigal of wonders than the art of being free is a truth that cannot be repeated too often" (*Democracy*, 2004, 275).

Tocqueville's love for freedom was more than personal. It was, in his view, emblematic of the democratic age in which he lived. "I think that democratic peoples have a natural taste for liberty. Left to themselves they seek it out, love it, and suffer if deprived of it." "Democracy" is a term with a special meaning in Tocqueville's writings. It describes a social situation rather than a political one, a social situation in which everyone is presumed to be equal. Democratic societies offer unique opportunities for freedom. Unfortunately, they also present special dangers for freedom, and much of Tocqueville's writing is devoted to the interplay between the two. Will democratic societies be ones in which people are equally free, or equally oppressed? Tocqueville devoted his writings to answering that question. Asking it meant that he was a "liberal of a new kind." He was a liberal in and of a democratic society, a man devoted to freedom in a world based on equality (*Democracy*, 2004, 584; *Reader*, 2002, 153).

Tocqueville rejects anything that he thinks threatens freedom, and supports anything he thinks encourages it. In freedom's name he rejects any form of omnipotence, whether exercised by a democratic majority or even by God, if that omnipotence should deny human free will. But in general Tocqueville saw no opposition between God and human freedom. Rather, he saw divine omnipotence as a necessary limit on human attempts to acquire omnipotence. Religion imposed limits on human action and belief that were essential to keeping humans free (*Democracy*, 2004, 337–40). One of the goals of *Democracy in America* was to show Europeans, and especially the French, that freedom and religion were natural allies, not natural enemies, despite what contemporary revolutionaries and reactionaries both claimed.

Tocqueville's commitment to freedom at its most absolute is expressed in his attitude towards freedom of the press: "among the moderns, the independence of the press is the most important, indeed the essential, ingredient of liberty. A people that wants to remain free therefore has the right to insist that the independence of the press be respected at all costs" (*Democracy*, 2004, 217). But Tocqueville is rarely so categorical in defending particular freedoms. Tocqueville opposed slavery, and unsuccessfully fought for its abolition in the French colonies, but the emancipation plans he supported were gradual ones. Even his defense of press freedom is tempered by "among the moderns." In other circumstances, things might be different. Freedom is essential. How freedom may best be preserved, created or extended is a question of time and circumstance. America may be the freest country on earth, nevertheless, those living in other countries, in other circumstances, are not advised to simply copy institutions that may not be appropriate for maintaining or establishing freedom elsewhere. Tocqueville's absolute commitment to certain ends, and his refusal to commit himself absolutely to any particular means, all the while emphasizing the importance of the means chosen, has sometimes perplexed his readers. But this is because it is all too easy to overlook the essential in Tocqueville because of the important role he gives the circumstantial.

Alongside his commitment to freedom there is another commitment essential to Tocqueville's thought: his commitment to France. His passion for France should never be underestimated. The reader should always bear in mind that, whatever Tocqueville is talking about, he is also talking about France – even when writing about democracy in America. As he wrote a friend, "although I very rarely spoke of France in [*Democracy in America*], I didn't write a page of it without thinking about France . . ." The freedom Tocqueville cares about most is French freedom (*OC*, 1977b, 209).

The patriotism and nationalism of nineteenth-century Europeans often looks overblown, or even hysterical, to their twenty-first-century descendants. Tocqueville's pride in his nation was intense. As he wrote in *The Old Regime*, "When I consider this nation [France] in itself, I find it more extraordinary than any of the events in its history." Even his contemporaries could be surprised by the depth of Tocqueville's feeling in this regard. The English philosopher John Stuart Mill was Tocqueville's friend. Mill's highly flattering reviews of *Democracy in America* in 1835 and 1840 (when its two volumes were published) did much to cement the friendship. But even such a friendly observer as Mill was shocked by Tocqueville's conduct during the Near Eastern Crisis of 1840–41, which brought France and England to the brink of war. Tocqueville gave a bellicose speech in the French assembly, and stunned Mill by writing him that "national pride is the greatest feeling which remains to us; doubtless it must be regulated and moderated in its excesses, but one must be careful not to lessen it." Tocqueville's pride in his country was such that he could not bear to see it give way in 1840, and would rather have fought a hopeless war against the rest of Europe (*OR*, 1998a, 246; *OC*, 1954, 330–31).

Often such strong nationalism has been at odds with the love of freedom, but this was never the case for Tocqueville, at least with regard to France. Divided in so many other ways, he was fortunate that in this, at least, he was able to reconcile his deepest impulses. For Tocqueville, France's glory was inseparable from its freedom, and whatever diminished the latter diminished the former. He would not trade freedom for power, regardless of the circumstances. He was equally hostile to Louis XIV and to Napoleon I. Freedom in France was Tocqueville's Holy Grail. All his writings are directly or indirectly dedicated to explaining how this might be achieved, or else to understanding why it was not. This is the essential Tocqueville.

How did Tocqueville come to think this way? Shortly after Tocqueville's death, the famous French literary critic Sainte-Beuve remarked of him that "he began to think before he knew anything" (Sainte-Beuve, 105n). But Sainte-Beuve was wrong. Before Tocqueville set foot aboard the boat to New York, he knew a lot, not about America, but about the problems he was going to America to solve, and the means he was going to use to solve them. As he wrote in a letter in 1835, "nearly ten years ago," that is, five years before he went to America, "I was already thinking about parts of the things I have just now set forth" (*SL*, 1985, 95). When he left for New York, Tocqueville already had in mind the outline of his analytic framework, an outline that owed much to others. Tocqueville's essential ideas and methods were based on those of many other thinkers. Before he arrived in America, Tocqueville's understanding of democracy, for all its originality, had been influenced by many people.

Tocqueville's intellectual tool-kit was extensive, and included contributions from a wide variety of sources. Some he admitted, on rare occasions in his works, more often in his letters. Others he passed over in silence. He was willing to acknowledge some intellectual debts, but not all. In the nineteenth century authors often did not cite their sources. Copious footnotes had not yet become a requirement for serious books. But Tocqueville took this practice to extremes.

It is characteristic of Tocqueville that when he did mention his predecessors by name, it was usually to establish his difference from them and assert his own originality. For example, in *The Old Regime and the Revolution* Tocqueville refers seven times to Edmund Burke, the great contemporary English commentator on the French Revolution. Once he agrees with him, once he uses him as reference for a fact and five times he cites him by name only to show how wrong he was. One would never guess from the references the enormous quantity of notes Tocqueville had made on Burke, nor the considerable intellectual debt he owed him (Gannett 57–78).

Montesquieu had even more influence on *Democracy in America* than Burke did on *The Old Regime*, but he is only mentioned by name three times, twice positively, once negatively. Rather than explicitly rejecting Montesquieu, Tocqueville criticizes him without directly referring to him. For example, in Tocqueville's discussion of the position of American women, he denies Montesquieu's well-known theory about the determining influence of climate on sexual mores and gender roles, without naming him. But more often than he rejects Montesquieu, Tocqueville borrows from him, beginning with the first chapter of the book, "The Outward Configuration of North America," a Montesquieu-like sketch of the influence of climate and geography on America's development.

Regardless of Tocqueville's silences, his sources can be discovered. They can be divided into two categories. The first category, more often acknowledged by Tocqueville, consists of seventeenth- and eighteenth-century writers. The second source of inspiration, rarely acknowledged even privately by Tocqueville, was his contemporaries.

In a letter written in 1836, just after the publication of the first volume of *Democracy in America*, Tocqueville wrote that "there are three men with whom I spend a little time every day, they are Pascal, Montesquieu and Rousseau." They are certainly the greatest influences from the past on Tocqueville, and arguably the most influential overall. Arguments about which individual was *most* important absorb many commentators, and usually tell us more about the commentator than about Tocqueville. If what matters most is the structure of Tocqueville's argument, the way in which he approaches a subject, then Montesquieu's *The Spirit of the Laws* is Tocqueville's guiding star. There are many ideas that Montesquieu and Tocqueville share. However, it is Tocqueville's characteristic style of explanation, his habit of explaining something one way, for instance by class, and then another way, by mores, and then a third way, by ideas or history, that he owes to Montesquieu. Even when addressing a question from just one of these perspectives, he was prone to argue both sides of an issue before coming to a nuanced conclusion. Mill described this as Tocqueville's "binocular" vision, which Mill defined as "seeing correctly because he [Tocqueville] saw the object in two positions at once, the angle of one point of vision correcting the obliquity of the other." As a result, just as Montesquieu has often been accused of contradiction, so has Tocqueville. Critics of Tocqueville should take to heart Montesquieu's response:

> When reading a book, we should be disposed to believe that the author has seen the contradictions that we imagine . . . When a work is systematic, we must still be sure we grasp the whole system. Look at a big machine made to produce an effect. You see wheels that turn in opposite directions; you would think on first glance that the machine was going to destroy itself . . . It keeps going; these pieces, which at first seem to be destroying each other, combine together for the proposed purpose. (Montesquieu, 2010, #2092)

So it is with Tocqueville. His work's deep structure has much in common with Montesquieu, and indeed from the publication of the first volume of *Democracy* in 1835 Tocqueville was hailed as a modern Montesquieu (*OC*, 1977a, 418; Mill in Mancini 25; Montesquieu, 2010, #2092).

Rousseau's influence on Tocqueville is less obvious, partly by accident, partly by design. In nineteenth-century France, Montesquieu was a respectable name, not so Rousseau. For many conservatives and moderates, Rousseau was the symbol of terror and bloodshed and everything wrong with the French Revolution. It would have done Tocqueville no good to associate himself with Rousseau. Unlike Montesquieu and Pascal, therefore, Rousseau is not mentioned by name in *Democracy in America*, and the single reference in *The Old Regime* is to the popularity of his literary style. Rousseau's traces are also harder for modern readers to see. Today, readers of Tocqueville are far more likely to associate Rousseau with *The Social Contract* than with the work that most influenced Tocqueville, *The Second Discourse*, also known as the *Discourse on Equality*. It is that work whose influence is most apparent in *Democracy* and Tocqueville's other writings, especially his "Memoir on Pauperism."

What Tocqueville borrows from Rousseau is both general and particular. In general, it is a fascination with the apparent paradoxes of equality. In particular, he borrows from Rousseau a whole series of insights into the psychology of human beings who live in democratic, that is egalitarian, societies. Tocqueville's anthropology and psychology probably owe more to Rousseau than to Montesquieu. Tocqueville's interest in the paradoxes of life in democratic society, where theoretically equal human beings constantly strive with one another for superiority, is Rousseauian. However, Tocqueville's insights into human psychology have diverse sources, sources whom it was more acceptable for Tocqueville to mention than Rousseau. In particular, rather than Rousseau, Tocqueville preferred to cite Pascal.

Tocqueville's relationship to Pascal's ideas was complicated. Pascal was one of the leading members of the seventeenth-century Catholic religious movement known as Jansenism. He was a devout Christian. Tocqueville, although deeply involved with religious issues, was not a Christian. Furthermore, Pascal's theology, like that of Jansenism in general, was fundamentally derived from St. Augustine, and made a sharp distinction between the concerns of this world and those of the next. Tocqueville was desperately trying to overcome the gap between the city of God and the city of this world. He wanted to make religion the ally of political freedom, not an indifferent stranger to it. While profoundly impressed by Pascal's insights into human nature (and those of other Jansenists, from the seventeenth to the nineteenth century), Tocqueville implicitly rejected a number of his views – just as he did in the case of Montesquieu and Rousseau. Pascal, after all, wrote that all humanity's troubles come from man's inability to sit quietly in a room (Pascal, #139). Tocqueville, devoted to political action, could hardly agree.

Nevertheless, Tocqueville's understanding of people owes much to Pascal's vision of the human condition. The greatness and misery of the human being described by Pascal bears a significant resemblance to the greatness and misery of democracy described by Tocqueville. Tocqueville the moralist owes as much to Pascal as Tocqueville the sociologist owes to Montesquieu. But of the three, it is Pascal whom Tocqueville most frequently cites with approval – he is mentioned by name four times in *Democracy*, always favorably, and many more times silently, albeit not always positively.

But if Tocqueville welcomed comparison with Montesquieu and did not disdain to mention Pascal, he was silent with respect to contemporary ideas. This is all the more striking because so many of them found a place in his work. It has been observed that Tocqueville's originality was created from other thinker's ideas. Many of the themes that have since become identified with Tocqueville were commonplaces of contemporary political debate and theory, if rarely so eloquently or coherently expressed. Tocqueville's work can be deconstructed as if it were a gigantic dictionary of commonplace ideas, like the one Flaubert started, but with special reference to politics and history. Part of Tocqueville's genius lay in applying commonplaces in new combinations and deploying them on new terrain, for example, America. His theories were constructed from a combination of other people's ideas and his own observation (Schlüter, 156).

Without giving a complete intellectual history of his time, certain contemporary influences on Tocqueville deserve particular mention. They can be divided into three groups: the Romantics, above all his elder cousin Chateaubriand; Catholic social thinkers, particularly Lamennais; and the "doctrinaire" political theorists, especially the man whose political role Tocqueville would despise above all others, Guizot. For all the influence the seventeenth and eighteenth centuries had on him, Tocqueville was a profoundly modern thinker, one who knew that anything written before the French Revolution would need significant updating to remain relevant afterwards.

Chateaubriand was the great literary lion of Tocqueville's youth. Many of Tocqueville's juvenile writings were attempts to imitate his style. But even the somewhat older Tocqueville, in *Democracy in America*, was not immune to writing passages about America's natural wonders strongly reminiscent of Chateaubriand's earlier efforts. Perhaps because of the strength of the attraction, Tocqueville made a deliberate effort to distinguish his writing from Chateaubriand's. Chateaubriand is, one commentator suggests, a kind of "literary father" whom Tocqueville must fight in order to establish his own existence (Guellec, 37). In *Democracy* Tocqueville often silently turns passages from Chateaubriand upside down. But the feeling for nature and the romantic/ pathetic tone sometimes to be found in Tocqueville's writing is a lasting inheritance from French Romanticism, from Rousseau to Chateaubriand.

The influence of Catholic thought on Tocqueville was until recently largely unrecognized, despite passages in his letters where Tocqueville speaks highly of such notable clerical writers as Bossuet, Bourdaloue, Lacordaire and Lamennais. Tocqueville was as familiar with their writings as he was with those of Pascal, Montesquieu and Rousseau. Lamennais' works in particular emphasized the close relationship between social structure, mores and religious beliefs. Many of Tocqueville's ideas on these questions have parallels in Lamennais' works, and indeed in that of the Catholic counter-revolutionary tradition as found in Maistre and Bonald. Tocqueville drew much from these writers, while coming to very different conclusions. Raised in a strongly Legitimist family, this circle of ideas was one in which he had grown up. But just as it was against his interest as an author to make much of Rousseau, for fear of appearing too far to the left, so it was in his interest to pass over these writers in silence, for fear of being identified with his family's royalism and conservatism (Jaume, chapter 2).

Guizot must be reckoned the most important of the contemporary influences on Tocqueville. He made an enormous impression on Tocqueville when Tocqueville came to Paris to start his legal studies. Tocqueville attended Guizot's lectures at the Sorbonne on French and European history and civilization, and read his historical works. In one letter he described Guizot's ability to analyze and describe ideas as "prodigious. "Guizot's analytic mind" became a synonym for brilliance in another letter. By Tocqueville's own admission Guizot opened his eyes to a whole new way of thinking about history, society and culture. He was astounded by the scope of what Guizot had to say. For the first time, it appears, Tocqueville became aware of how it was possible to analyze all kinds of historical actions and ideas within an account of the development of a single principle, for example, democracy. Along with Guizot, others of the same "doctrinaire" school of political thought, notably Rémusat, whom Tocqueville later feared would write his *Old Regime* before him, so similar were their ideas in many respects, helped Tocqueville formulate the questions he took to America with him. Even if Tocqueville rejected the doctrinaires' vision of the middle class as the ruling class, even if he would later cover Guizot with contempt as the example of all that was corrupt in France, Guizot and the doctrinaires' "prodigious" example contributed much to the methods followed by Tocqueville in *Democracy in America* (*OC*, 1967a, 80; Craiutu).

The close connection between Tocqueville's ideas and those of his contemporaries, even when he rejected them, is one of the ways in which Tocqueville never stopped thinking about France, even when he was in America writing about democracy. There is always a layer of meaning in Tocqueville's writing that is addressed to particular issues confronting France. When he talks about the relationship between religion and the state in America, for example, the relationship between throne and altar in France is much on his mind.

Tocqueville is rarely read today for the purpose of understanding early-nineteenth-century France, and of course this is not surprising. But without knowing something about nineteenth-century France, it will be difficult to understand Tocqueville. The most important thing to recognize about Tocqueville's France, in this context, is that it was a post-revolutionary society, indeed, the model post-revolutionary society. One thing Tocqueville learned from his contemporaries, something he could never learn from the past, were the questions confronting a society in transition, in transition between one form of society and another as well as between one form of government and another. This set of peculiarly modern questions, posed again and again in the decades and centuries to come, was an important part of Tocqueville's intellectual equipment when he set sail for America.

Tocqueville may have known almost nothing about America when he left France, but he had done a great deal of thinking about what he did know, and what he wanted to find out. In America, he learned much.

3

Democracy and Freedom in America

There are three things commentators feel compelled to say about *Democracy in America*. One is that it is a book that appeals to both the left and the right. The second is that it is the most widely quoted book about the United States ever written. The third is that it is the best book ever written about America. All three statements are equally true, and perhaps equally remarkable – and perhaps the first is the cause of the second and third. The fact that they are true shows that Tocqueville succeeded in using the ideas and methods he had brought with him and transforming them into a new and unprecedented analysis of both democracy and America.

Part of the reason for his success was that if his ideas were largely old, his methods of applying them were new. Comparison was at the heart of his approach. Of course, people had been writing about the faraway places they had visited long before Tocqueville. They naturally compared the places they had been with the places they had come from. But for Tocqueville, the comparative method was absolutely central to understanding not just America, but France, Europe and modernity. Comparing France and America is at the heart of *Democracy*, but it is not the only comparison Tocqueville makes. America is compared to France, but also to England and Russia. The different regions of America are compared to one another. The typical American individual is compared to the typical French person. Democracy is compared to aristocracy.

Few other thinkers have been so relentlessly comparative in their analyses.

But Tocqueville did not just observe and compare and report the results. He used his observations and comparisons to create a new kind of sociological method that Max Weber would later popularize as the construction of "ideal types." Out of the many individuals he encountered, Tocqueville constructed a general image of the human condition in democratic society, the democratic man (and the democratic woman, too). He differentiated the subset of the American from this archetype. The American was democratic, but also possessed his/her own national and regional peculiarities. In his account, Tocqueville used ideal types to embody the psychology produced by larger social forces. He could thus describe how individuals felt and acted in democratic societies, and how Americans in particular felt and acted. Tocqueville used his comparative method and his ideal types to create a picture of democracy and of America that has never been surpassed. In *Democracy in America* we find a picture of America, a picture of democracy and, most important of all in Tocqueville's view, a description of the threats freedom faced in America and elsewhere and the remedies the Americans had found for them.

It is crucial to recognize that democracy and America are two things in Tocqueville's account, not one. *Democracy in America* is a book *about* democracy. America is the setting, not the subject. However, in order to distinguish between what was true of democracy as a social state, and what was particular to the American setting, Tocqueville had to pay careful attention to America. He also wanted to pay careful attention to America because at the time America was the closest thing to a pure example of democracy in the world. In many respects it still is, and this is one reason for the enduring fascination of Tocqueville's work.

In order to understand *Democracy in America*, one must understand the most basic, simplest and most difficult concept in the book: democracy. What does Tocqueville mean by "democracy"?

More than one thing, and sometimes more than one thing at the same time.[1]

What confuses modern readers is that for Tocqueville the fundamental meaning of "democracy" is not political. He speaks about it as a social state in which conditions are equal. This is almost equally confusing, because contemporary readers think he means economic conditions when what he really means is that in democracies social status is, at least in theory, equal. Democracy is a social system based on equality. A democratic world is one in which people assume that everyone is the equal of everyone else. Often the easiest way to understand a word is by learning its antonym. The antonym for "democracy," in this sense, is "aristocracy," a social system based on hereditary ranks in which everyone has subordinates and superiors.[2] *Democracy in America* is a book about what life is like when people are equals, when they live their lives surrounded by people they consider in principle to be no better or worse than themselves. In democratic societies people may not have the same amount of money, or brains, or beauty, but they expect to be treated as the moral and legal and social equals of everyone else, whose opinions deserve equal respect. They are addressed with the same titles (such as Mr), they are able to marry whomever will agree to marry them, they are subject to the same laws and their souls are presumed to be of equal worth in the eyes of God. Difference is the exception, not the rule, and must be justified, whereas in an aristocratic society, difference is the rule, and it is equality that is the exception and requires special justification.

In the twenty-first century, this is our world, and it is hard for us to imagine anything else. In 1835, when Tocqueville published the first volume of *Democracy*, or in 1840, when he published the

---

[1] The most complete discussion of the meaning of "democracy" in *Democracy in America*, suggesting fourteen different uses of the word, will be found in Schleifer (2000, chapter 19).

[2] For a discussion of the concept of aristocracy in Tocqueville, useful for a full understanding of its antonym democracy, see Kahan (2007, 324–48).

second, this was not the case. All Europeans (and most other peoples) lived in societies that were either aristocratic or in a transitional stage between aristocracy and democracy. America was exceptional in that it was, as Tocqueville saw it, a fully democratic society that had never experienced aristocracy.[3] "Things are different in America . . . In America, democracy is left to its own propensities. Its manner is natural and its movement free. There is where it must be judged" (*Democracy*, 2004a, 224).

Tocqueville was obsessed by democracy in America because he realized that democracy was the fate of France, and indeed of the whole world. "A great democratic revolution is taking place among us," "wherever we look in the Christian world, we see the same ongoing revolution," Tocqueville wrote. "There is no doubt in my mind that sooner or later we will come, as the Americans have come, to an almost complete equality of conditions" (3, 14).

Unlike political revolutions, accomplished in a short period of time, this democratic revolution had been going on for centuries. For centuries, aristocratic social institutions had been in decline. The conclusion to be drawn was clear: "I am firmly of the opinion that the democratic revolution to which we are witness is an irresistible fact, and one that it would be neither desirable nor wise to oppose . . ." Indeed, democracy is God's will. Tocqueville was inspired with religious awe in considering it: "This entire book was written in the grip of a kind of religious terror occasioned in the soul of the author by the sight of this irresistible revolution, which for centuries now has surmounted every obstacle . . . To wish to arrest democracy would then seem tantamount to a struggle against God himself . . ." Was Tocqueville expressing a religious conviction, or merely trying to convince conservative French Catholics to give up a hopeless fight? Regardless, the point Tocqueville is making is clear: Democracy is inevitable. Don't fight it. It will soon be self-evident that all human beings are created equal (6–7).

---

[3] With the exception of slavery; see pp. 54-6.

Is this good news? Tocqueville admitted that from God's perspective it is.

It is natural to believe that what is most satisfying to the eye of man's creator and keeper is not the singular prosperity of a few but the greater well-being of all: what seems decadence to me is therefore progress in his eyes; what pains me pleases him. Equality is less lofty, perhaps, but more just, and its justice is the source of its grandeur and beauty. (833)

Democracy is inevitable. It is more just than aristocracy. But will it be free? Tocqueville always comes back to his essential question: What does democracy mean for freedom, and especially for French freedom? In examining democracy in America, Tocqueville was looking for lessons from which Europe might profit. However, Tocqueville did not mean to suggest that other countries simply copy what worked in the United States. "Anyone who, after reading this book, concludes that my goal in writing it was to suggest that every people whose social state is democratic ought to mimic the mores of the Americans is guilty of a serious error." France had a different history and a different society than America. Therefore, the mores appropriate for France would be different. Every nation will one day be as democratic as America, but every nation must find its own path to the freedom Americans enjoy – and this is a good thing. Tocqueville was an early friend of diversity: "I should regard it as a great misfortune for the human race if liberty were obliged to exhibit identical features wherever it manifests itself" (364).

The question of how to combine democracy with freedom leads us to the other sense in which Tocqueville uses the term "democracy," its political sense. The word "democracy" in Tocqueville is like an accordion, it stretches and contracts depending on the notes Tocqueville wants to play. The context is important for understanding the word, but not always sufficient. The word always means equality. In addition, it sometimes means a particular form of government. Tocqueville slides back and forth among the uses of the term, sometimes in rapid succession. Often the signal that he is talking about politics is the phrase "democratic institutions." It is only the combination of democratic political institutions with a democratic society that can lead to freedom in the modern world.

Both meanings of the term matter, and it is the combination of the two that helps explain why Tocqueville went to America. Not just to study democracy as a social state, but to study how democracy could be combined with a lasting freedom. The fact that the United States had lasted, and remained free, that the thirteen colonies had not degenerated into a bunch of squabbling dictatorships, as so many other postcolonial regimes had done in nineteenth-century Latin America, and would do in twentieth-century Africa and Asia, was central to America's attraction for Tocqueville. "The democratic republic in the United States continues to exist. The principal purpose of this book has been to explain the cause of this phenomenon."[4] It was a question that mattered to "the entire world; not just one nation, but all mankind" (360).

The basic problem that Tocqueville confronted was stated in one of his chapter titles: "Why Democratic Peoples Show a More Ardent and Enduring Love of Equality than of Liberty." As he put it, "The taste that men have for liberty and the one they feel for equality are in fact two distinct things, and I do not shrink from adding that in democratic nations they are two unequal things." Equality is far more attractive to most people in democratic societies. The reasons for this have to do with both perception and reality. "The goods that liberty yields reveal themselves only in the long run, and it is always easy to mistake their cause. The advantages of equality are felt immediately and can be seen to flow daily from their source." It is hard for people to recognize, for example, that their long-term economic prosperity is

---

[4] The reader should not take the statement "principal purpose of this book" too seriously. Tocqueville repeats it several times about several different things. See *Democracy* (2004, 319 and 330).

due to their political freedom, easy for them to put it down to other causes and easy for them to see, by contrast, when political freedom leads to short-term economic problems. By contrast, people recognize the benefits of equality immediately, whether they be in the form of rights or cash or polite forms of address. It is rather the "ills that extreme equality can produce [which] reveal themselves only a little at a time." The benefits of freedom are long-term, while those of equality are immediate. The costs of freedom are immediate, while the cost of equality is often hard to perceive, and those who do perceive it "know that the miseries they fear are remote and are pleased to think that they will afflict only future generations, for which the present generation evinces little concern." Equality is thus no guarantee of freedom: "It is easy to imagine . . . hypothetical situations in which a significant degree of equality would be comfortably combined with more or less free institutions or even with institutions that were not free at all." The problem of combining equality and freedom, democracy and liberty, is at the heart of *Democracy in America*, and at the heart of all Tocqueville's work. Tocqueville knew the future would be democratic. He did not know if it would be free (581–82).

Part of the reason that the future of political freedom was unclear, in Tocqueville's view, was that while in the long run everyone does benefit from political freedom, in the short run its benefits are not just hard to perceive, they are restricted to a relative few: "To a certain number of citizens political liberty gives sublime pleasures from time to time. Equality provides a multitude of lesser pleasures to everyone every day." Here Tocqueville comes close to reserving the pleasures of freedom to an elite. In a democratic age, this amounts to something perilously near a death sentence. Hence he hastens to add that "democratic peoples have a natural taste for liberty. Left to themselves, they seek it out, love it, and suffer if deprived of it." After reading this chapter one is tempted to ask why they should care.

Democracy in America was written partly to answer this very question. It is an explication of the fact "that nothing is more prodigal of wonders than the art of being free." America is essential to Tocqueville as living proof of what would otherwise be the dubious proposition that freedom and equality can coexist, and that this is good. But America also illustrates that liberty is second to equality among democratic passions. People "want equality in liberty, and if they cannot have it, they want it still in slavery."[5] Over the course of his life Tocqueville slowly moved from optimism about the future of freedom to pessimism. In *Democracy in America* he is, on the whole, an optimist (275, 583–84).

In Tocqueville's optimistic moods, he focuses on the ways in which equality fosters freedom. "Equality, which makes men independent of one another, fosters the habit of and taste for governing their course in private actions solely by their own will . . . Men who live in such times therefore proceed with a natural bias toward free institutions." Tocqueville's admiration for equality's justice is somewhat forced, however. As he wrote in a note to himself, "I have an intellectual preference for democratic institutions, but I am aristocratic by instinct, that is I despise and fear the crowd." When equality led to freedom, however, Tocqueville's enthusiasm for democracy was unfeigned. "I admire equality when I see it deposit an obscure notion of, and instinctive penchant for, political independence in every man's heart and mind, thereby preparing the remedy for the ill that it provokes. It is this aspect of equality that I hold dear." But Tocqueville also saw that "Equality in fact produces two tendencies . . ." one to freedom, the other to despotism. The path between equality and freedom is more direct, but "a longer, more hidden but also more certain path [leads] to servitude." Tocqueville went so far as to claim that "it is easier to establish an absolute and despotic government in a nation where conditions are equal than in any other . . ." (787–88; *Reader*, 2002, 219).

---

[5] It would be interesting to write a history of Communism as a commentary on this passage.

In *Democracy in America* it was Tocqueville's task to explain the choice between despotism and freedom democracy faced, to explore the choices Americans had made and to understand what lessons America could and could not teach France and the rest of the world. The first volume (1835) is more concrete, more oriented towards the peculiarities of America. The reader looking for Tocqueville's descriptions of Jacksonian America will find most of them there. The second volume (1840) is more abstract, more oriented towards analyzing democracy in general. As Tocqueville said while writing it, "now I can see almost the whole book, and I realize that it is much more about the general effects of equality on mores than about the particular effects it produces in America" (*OC*, 1970, 71). Scholars debate the relationship between the two volumes. Are they really two books, perhaps with contrasting conclusions, or just one work, more or less coherent? Readers will have their own answers to this question. As one commentator puts it, "there are no absolutists in this debate." Tocqueville's understanding of democracy changed between the two volumes of the *Democracy*, but in the manner of someone proceeding up a spiral staircase, he kept circling the same core issues. The essential Tocqueville remains unchanged over time; his preoccupations with freedom and with France never vary (Schleifer 1992, 194).

Exploring these issues, Tocqueville painted a pair of parallel portraits, democracy alongside America. He looked at both of them from every perspective he could imagine. *Democracy in America* analyzes the general problems posed by democracy in an American context, as well as distinctively American problems in their democratic context. Examples of the former discussed later are Tocqueville's discussions of the tyranny of the majority, individualism, materialism and centralization, and the remedies the Americans applied to all these ills. An example of a peculiarly American problem Tocqueville studied is slavery, to which neither the Americans of his day nor Tocqueville had any remedy.

Of all the threats to freedom described in *Democracy in America*, "the tyranny of the majority" is probably the most notorious.

Although it comes from the second part of volume one, it makes a good place to begin discussing the relationship between the two meanings of "democracy," that is, between equality and political freedom. This is because the "tyranny of the majority" requires both a democratic society, since otherwise the majority would not have much influence, and a democratic government, since otherwise they would not be able to exercise their influence. The majority rules in democracy. This is not tyrannical in itself. The problem is that "liberty is imperiled if that power meets with no obstacle capable of slowing its advance and giving it time to moderate itself." In America, the majority is omnipotent, according to Tocqueville. It is omnipotent in politics, through frequent elections by universal suffrage. Even more important, in Tocqueville's eyes, is "the power that the majority in America exercises over thought." He continued:

> It is when one comes to examine the way in which thought is exercised in the United States that one perceives quite clearly the degree to which the power of the majority exceeds all the powers we are acquainted with in Europe . . . I know of no country where there is in general less independence of mind and true freedom of discussion than in America. (*Democracy*, 2004, 289, 293)

For Tocqueville, omnipotence was "a bad and dangerous thing" in any hands other than God's. The fact that omnipotence was exercised by the majority in the name of equality did nothing to justify it. "There is no authority on earth so inherently worthy of respect, or invested with a right so sacred, that I would want to let it act without oversight or rule without impediment." With the coming of democratic society and democratic government, tyranny changed shape, but was no less menacing than it had been when exercised by a king. America, as Tocqueville described it, showed how that threat might take shape. However, Tocqueville pointed out, "I am not saying that recourse to tyranny is frequent in America today, only that no guarantee against it can be found, and that the reasons for the mildness of government must be sought in the circumstances and mores rather than in the laws." As medieval medical theory dictated, if God placed a disease in a certain place, he placed the remedy near to hand. If America displayed the tyranny of the majority, she also showed how that tyranny might be remedied (290–91, 298).

The tyrannical potential of democratic government represents a threat to freedom imposed from above. Majority tyranny exercised by democratic society represents a threat to freedom from below. Individualism represents a threat to freedom from inside, from the psychology of the individual in a democratic society. "Individualism," like "democracy," is a word that Tocqueville gives a particular meaning to. Unlike "democracy," however, he provides a concise definition of what it means: "Individualism is a reflective and tranquil sentiment that disposes each citizen to cut himself off from the mass of his fellow men and withdraw into the circle of family and friends, so that, having created a little society for his own use, he gladly leaves the larger society to take care of itself." When people are individualistic in this way, they are not exactly selfish, since they do care about some other people. But they do not care about society as a whole. Individualism does not exist, according to Tocqueville, in aristocratic societies, since in such societies everyone has strong links to those above and below them in the social hierarchy. In democracies, by contrast, everyone feels independent and equal to everyone else. This is why "Individualism is democratic in origin, and it threatens to develop as conditions equalize" (585).

Why does this concern Tocqueville? Because individualism is a powerful encouragement for despotism. The individualist "exists only in himself and for himself, and if he still has a family, he no longer has a country." The democratic despot will encourage individualism in order to maintain power:

I am trying to imagine what new features despotism might have in today's world: I see an innumerable host of men, all

equal and alike, endlessly hastening after petty and vulgar
pleasures with which they fill their souls. Each of them, withdrawn into himself, is virtually a stranger to the fate of all the
others. For him, his children and personal friends comprise
the entire human race. As for the remainder of his fellow
citizens, he lives alongside them but does not see them. (818)

In a world of individualists, freedom will find few friends, and
despots will find few willing to take the trouble to oppose them,
as long as things are orderly. Apathy is the natural political state
of the individualist (869).

Individualism also encourages, and is in turn encouraged by,
another common feature of democratic societies that America
displays prominently: the passion for material well-being.
Democracy leaves human souls "inordinately vulnerable to material pleasures." Tocqueville was no ascetic. He had nothing
against material well-being in itself, but rather, "I reproach
equality not for leading men into the pursuit of forbidden pleasure but for absorbing them entirely in the search for permitted
ones." America is a particularly good playground for materialism, because of the unprecedented opportunities it offers for
making money. In America, "the possibilities open to greed are
endlessly breathtaking, and the human mind, constantly dis-
tracted from the pleasures of the imagination and the works of
the intellect, is engaged solely by the pursuit of wealth." The
universal desire for material well-being is democratic, but its
strength in America is multiplied by the fact that "the situation
of the American is entirely exceptional, and there is reason to
believe that no other democratic people will ever enjoy anything
like it" (503, 516–17, 622).

Tocqueville devotes several chapters of the second volume of
Democracy to "The Taste for Material Well-Being in America,"
"The Particular Effects of the Love of Material Gratifications in
Democratic Countries" and "How the Taste for Material Gratifi-
cations is Combined in America with Love of Liberty and
Concern About Public Affairs," the latter being a discussion of

the remedies the Americans have found for the tendency of people in democratic societies to care only about how much money they can make. Tocqueville is, as always, concerned about the effects materialism will have on freedom. He is also deeply troubled by how the combination of individualism with materialism in democratic society will lead to a degradation of the human character, the spread of mediocrity and the decline of all forms of greatness. In his opinion the Americans had only partly remedied this problem (617–22, 629–32).

All these threats – the tyranny of the majority, individualism, materialism – come to a head in one of the central themes of Tocqueville's work, the problem of centralization. A strong, centralized government is a perfect instrument for the tyranny of the majority, "and fear of disorder and love of well-being imperceptibly lead democratic peoples to increase the prerogatives of the central government, the only power that seems to them sufficiently strong, sufficiently intelligent, and sufficiently stable to protect them from anarchy" (801). The more centralization, the less freedom.

Centralization, it would seem, is a bad thing according to Tocqueville. But once again we must not oversimplify him, because sooner or later he will make a subtle distinction. Tocqueville distinguishes between governmental centralization, a good thing, and administrative centralization, a bad thing. Governmental centralization has to do with "the enactment of general laws and relations with foreigners." It concerns things of equal interest to the whole country that ought to be decided in one place by a government sufficiently strong to enforce its decisions. Administrative centralization has to do with matters of local interest. It is bad when such matters are ruled from a faraway capital. "In some respects the distinction between the two kinds of centralization becomes blurred. But if we consider the totality of matters falling specifically within the purview of each, we can easily distinguish them." It is also true that "these two types of centralization support each other and share a mutual attraction, but I cannot believe they are inseparable" (97–98).

But even if they are separable in theory, in practice it was hard to separate them in democracies. "As conditions in a nation become more equal, individuals appear smaller and society seems greater, or, rather, each citizen, having become just like all the others, is lost in the crowd, until nothing can be seen any more but the vast and magnificent image of the people itself," embodied in the government. Democratic societies are naturally inclined to favor centralization. "In the democratic centuries that are about to begin, I think that individual independence and local liberties will always be a product of art. Centralization will be the natural form of government" (790).

But nature is not destiny for Tocqueville. Human art can oppose nature. Centralization can thus be successfully fought, even in democratic societies, partly because "centralization in a democratic nation develops in accord not only with the progress of equality but also with the way in which equality is established." Their history led the French to think that local independence was a bad thing. Tocqueville put this down to ignorance in sentences directed at his countrymen: "Only peoples among whom provincial institutions are entirely or almost entirely nonexistent deny their usefulness. In other words, the only people who speak ill of such institutions are those who know nothing about them." America was a good place to look for the remedy for centralization, too (109–10, 796, 798).

How then did the Americans manage to combine freedom and democracy in the face of such daunting threats as centralization, individualism, materialism and the tyranny of the majority? The Americans had found remedies, but unfortunately their remedies were often regarded with hostility or perceived as threats by the French of Tocqueville's day. In particular Tocqueville stressed the role of associations, enlightened self-interest and religion in America. And above all, a remedy that many Frenchmen were especially inclined to distrust: "I maintain," wrote Tocqueville, "that to combat the evils that equality may engender, there is only one effective remedy: political liberty." Freedom is both the base and the crown of the edifice (594).

In democracies, where everyone is equal, and all individuals equally powerless against the majority, association is the only means by which individuals can effectively exercise their freedom. Association is one of the rare subjects Tocqueville treats at length in both volumes of *Democracy* – a sign of its importance, both to America and to democracy. "No country in the world has made better use of association than the United States, and nowhere has that powerful instrument been applied to a wider range of purposes." In Europe, political and even private associations were feared, and with reason, Tocqueville admitted, as potential agents of revolution. But "it is sometimes the case that extreme freedom corrects the abuses of freedom and extreme democracy guards against the dangers of democracy." In America, political associations were tamed by universal suffrage, which meant that no association could claim to speak for a silent majority. Thus tamed, "freedom of association has become a necessary guarantee against the tyranny of the majority." Association is America's sovereign remedy against democracy's dangers. "If men are to remain civilized, or to become so, they must develop and perfect the art of associating to the same degree that equality of conditions increases among them" (215, 218, 222).

Political activity is, for Tocqueville, the fundamental associative act from which all others follow, and politics is the means by which people are taught to associate: "Political associations [are] vast free schools to which all citizens come to learn the general theory of association." Tocqueville did not urge that Europe (in particular France) copy the unlimited freedom of political association he found in America. It would be too dangerous. Nevertheless, freedom of association is precious in Tocqueville's eyes. It is a crucial component of American freedom. Association provides the counterweight to government that would otherwise be missing in a democratic society. "Nowhere are associations more necessary to prevent either the despotism of the parties or the arbitrariness of the prince than in countries whose social state is democratic." As the aristocracy had once limited the ruler's power, so association creates a sort of artificial aristocracy:

"ordinary citizens, by associating, can constitute very opulent, very influential, and very powerful entities – in a word, they can play the role of aristocrats" (219, 606, 824).[6]

Once taught to associate in politics, people soon learn to associate for other purposes. The practice of association combats individualism by encouraging isolated individuals to join together to achieve their goals. "Wherever there is a new undertaking, at the head of which you would expect to see in France the government and in England some great lord, in the United States you are sure to find an association." Tocqueville titles a crucial chapter, "How Americans Combat Individualism with Free Institutions." Thus, "the Americans have used liberty to combat the individualism born of equality, and they have defeated it" (590, 591, 595, 599).

Tocqueville used his account of America to send a message to France and to the world: It is in the self-interest of democratic people to associate, and of free governments to let them. In the idea and practice of enlightened self-interest itself Tocqueville saw another remedy against the threats that democracy poses to freedom. He titles another chapter, "How Americans Combat Individualism with the Doctrine of Self-Interest Properly Understood" (610). But what does Tocqueville mean by "properly understood"?

A proper understanding of one's interest means taking a broad, long-term view. For example, a businessman willing to pay higher taxes to support better schools, because this will mean better-educated workers, is displaying enlightened self-interest. This enlightened perspective is widespread in the United States. "Americans . . . will obligingly demonstrate how enlightened love of themselves regularly leads them to help one another out and makes them ready and willing to sacrifice a portion of their time and wealth for the good of the state."

---

[6] Tocqueville makes a similar argument about the role of the American judicial system in countering the tyranny of the majority. See *Democracy* (2004, 111–19, 825–26).

Doing so is useful – to themselves. Utility is the democratic criterion of value *par excellence.* That is why for Tocqueville "the doctrine of self-interest properly understood seems to me the most appropriate to the needs of my contemporaries . . ." Furthermore, it is one they can understand. "Self-interest properly understood is not a very lofty doctrine, but it is a clear and reliable one . . . Since it is within the reach of every intelligence, anyone can grasp it easily and retain it without difficulty" (611–12).

However, the doctrine of enlightened self-interest is not wholly a good thing in Tocqueville's eyes. Self-interest properly understood helps people to overcome their individualism, it discourages crime, but if it makes people better human beings, it does not lead them to become great ones.

> If the doctrine of self-interest properly understood were ever to achieve total domination of the moral world, extraordinary virtues would no doubt become more rare, but crude depravity would, I think, also become less common . . . Consider a few individuals and the doctrine brings them down. Think of the species and the doctrine raises it up. (612)

It sometimes seems as if everything is for the best in Tocqueville's democratic world, but this is not the case. Democracy is inevitable, it is just, but it is not and cannot be perfect. Tocqueville will not try to make democratic society or democratic people achieve great virtues that go against their grain.

Tocqueville refuses to try to perform the impossible. He tries to persuade his contemporaries likewise: "No power on earth can prevent growing equality of conditions from prompting the human mind to investigate what is useful or from disposing individual citizens to turn inward on themselves." Individualism is inevitable. All that can be done is to enlighten self-interest in order to combat it. "Enlighten them, therefore, regardless of the cost, for the century of blind self-sacrifice and instinctive virtue is fast receding into the past, and what I see approaching is an

age in which liberty, public peace, and social order itself will be
unable to do without enlightenment" (613).

Enlightened self-interest brings together opposites such as
selfishness and altruism. Its magic extends to making democracy
and religion partners instead of enemies. From the perspective
of many nineteenth-century Frenchmen, this was squaring the
circle. The idea that religion could be combined with enlightenment, or with support for equality, or for democratic political
institutions, seemed laughable. Nevertheless, a chapter title
reads: "How the Americans Apply the Doctrine of Self-Interest
Properly Understood in the Matter of Religion." The idea was
not a new one. Pascal, Tocqueville noted, had already instructed
people that it was in their interest to wager on the truth of
Christianity. In America, religion often replaced the heavenly
reward on which Pascal had based his wager with more earthly
motives:

> American preachers refer to this world constantly and, indeed,
> can avert their eyes from it only with the greatest of difficulty.
> Seeking to touch their listeners all the more effectively, they
> are forever pointing out how religious beliefs foster liberty
> and public order, and in listening to them it is often difficult
> to tell whether the chief object of religion is to procure eternal
> happiness in the other world or well-being in this one. (616)

In democratic America, religion and enlightened self-interest
mix. To this argument Tocqueville added others, more surprising yet to many of his contemporaries, about the way in which
religion and freedom were natural allies in a democracy, rather
than natural enemies. "In New England, . . . education and liberty are the daughters of morality and religion." Nothing was
more surprising in Paris (228, 614–16).

It is difficult to overestimate the importance of religion in
Tocqueville's analysis of *Democracy in America*. Of all the supports
for freedom the Americans had found, it is perhaps the one
Tocqueville stressed most, if only because it was most surprising

to a French audience. Like association, it is one of the few topics discussed at length in both volumes. If we recall that at one point he identified the persistence of a democratic republic in the United States as the key question in the *Democracy*, then this section title takes on its full significance: "On Religion Considered as a Political Institution: How Mightily it Contributes to the Persistence of the Democratic Republic among the Americans." Tocqueville knew that in Europe, and above all in France, religion, that is, Catholicism, had been the enemy of both freedom and equality. But in a democratic society freedom needs religion as an ally, and vice versa (332).

America is Tocqueville's proof. Tocqueville called America the world's most Christian nation. He concluded from this that "there is no better illustration of the usefulness and naturalness of religion, since the country where its influence is greatest today is also the country that is freest and most enlightened." In America, everyone thought that religion was democracy's friend, and no one argued that they were natural enemies. Tocqueville argued that religion was a necessary support for morality, and perhaps the sole weapon remaining to democracies against materialism. He devoted a chapter to discussing "How Religious Beliefs Sometimes Divert the American Soul toward Immaterial Gratification." Which religious beliefs sometimes appear not to matter: "Most religions are merely general, simple, and practical means of teaching men the immortality of the soul. This is the greatest benefit that a democratic people can derive from its beliefs, and it is what makes beliefs more necessary to such a people than to all others," for without it, materialism and individualism are likely to be all-conquering (336, 635).

But if any religion is better than none, there was one religion to which Tocqueville devoted more attention than any other, the dominant religion not of America, but of France: Catholicism. One of his least prophetic chapters was "On the Progress of Catholicism in the United States," in which he predicted a Catholic future for America. Did Tocqueville believe in this prediction himself? He probably did not much care. His goal was to show conservative French Catholics and radical French atheists that war was not the natural relationship between Catholicism and democracy, and that it was not fate that bound throne and altar together. At several points in the *Democracy* Tocqueville argues that Catholicism is more egalitarian than Protestantism, and that it can be freedom's ally. The key condition for this is the separation of church and state. Tocqueville deliberately brings the favorable testimony of several American Catholic priests to bear on this point, in order to emphasizes as strongly as possible that this separation strengthens not merely the state, but the Church: "to a man, they [Catholic priests] assigned primary credit for the peaceful ascendancy of religion in their country to the complete separation of church and state. I state without hesitation that during my stay in America I met no one – not a single clergyman or layman – who did not agree with this statement" (332, 341, 510).

Through association, enlightened self-interest and religion, America fought the threats to freedom posed by democracy. All are themselves eminently democratic means, or at least not anti-democratic. Although decentralization, a political artifact, aids their function, the remedies are chiefly examples of the power of *mores* to influence society. By "mores" Tocqueville means the "moral and intellectual state of a people." These, for him, are more important than the laws or the political institutions, even if the latter are important too. "Laws do more to maintain a democratic republic in the United States than physical causes do, and mores do more than laws." The mores of Americans are those of a democratic people who have never known aristocracy. Even more importantly, they are those of a free people. If others cannot imitate their history, they can still emulate their freedom (331, 352).

But there is one respect in which American mores were opposed to freedom, and which presented a peculiarly American challenge to democracy. No commentator on democracy in America could avoid talking about the anomaly that slavery presented. Slavery was an institution both aristocratic and despotic.

Tocqueville opposed it. In his political career, he fought unsuccessfully to abolish it in the French colonies. In America, he was a keen observer of the ways in which the democratic character was influenced by slavery in the slave-owning South. Dealing with the institution of slavery and with the slaves themselves was the greatest challenge America faced: "The most redoubtable of all the ills that threaten the future of the United States stems from the presence of Blacks on its soil." The association of slavery with race was central to the problem that slavery posed to America, as Tocqueville recognized. He foresaw a future of blood and tears, in which "great woes certainly lie ahead" (392, 419).

Racial integration was not on the horizon in America in 1835. In prescient words, written long before the Civil War abolished slavery but maintained racial discrimination in the United States, Tocqueville wrote that "If Whites are to give up their belief in the intellectual and moral inferiority of their former slaves, the Negroes must change, but they cannot change so long as this belief persists." His conclusion was that "those who hope that the Negroes will one day blend in with the Europeans are nursing a chimera." What then? Tocqueville quoted Thomas Jefferson's words that it was inevitable that the slaves would one day be free, but impossible that they should live alongside Whites as equals. One solution, that of Latin America, was intermarriage and the disappearance of the Black population into the White by dilution. Tocqueville did not oppose this, but he did not see it as a solution likely to be adopted in the United States. Since they would not marry Black people, since they would not accept them as equals, slave-owners were condemned to keep Blacks as slaves (394n.32, 395, 411, 411n.46).

Tocqueville's attitude had much in common with that of Abraham Lincoln. Tocqueville and Lincoln both foretold the eventual disappearance of slavery. Both rejected its extension to new territories (Tocqueville's letters to his American correspondents in the 1850s are very firm on this point). Neither, before the Civil War, favored its forced abolition on American soil. And neither accepted its right to exist. "God forbid that I should try to justify the principle of Negro servitude, as some American authors do," wrote Tocqueville. Lincoln similarly invoked the divine during the Civil War, in his Second Inaugural Address:

> If God wills that [the war] continue until all the wealth piled by the bondsman's two hundred and fifty years of unrequited toil shall be sunk, and until every drop of blood drawn by the lash shall be paid by another drawn with the sword, as was said three thousand years ago, so still it must be said, "The judgments of the Lord are true and righteous altogether."

Tocqueville had prophesied freedom for the Blacks, thirty years before it came. He also foresaw civil war between Blacks and Whites – which, if one considers the history of Black people in America from the Reconstruction period after 1865 to the Civil Rights Movement of the 1960s, is perhaps not the least accurate of his predictions (416).

The picture Tocqueville drew of democracy in America, the threats it presented and the remedies the Americans had found, was intended to be a plan of action for the future as much as it was a description of the present. In neither respect was it without flaws. His use of the word "democracy" itself was perhaps overbroad. In reviewing the second volume, John Stuart Mill complained that Tocqueville took everything modern and called it "democracy." Tocqueville had answered this objection in *Democracy* itself: "Because I attribute such a variety of effects to equality, the reader might conclude that I regard it as the sole cause of everything that happens nowadays. But to do so would be to assume that I hold a very narrow view indeed" (479). Despite Tocqueville's disclaimer, there is some truth in the objection. There are also many well-founded objections to details in the work, and many of Tocqueville's prophecies turned out to be inaccurate.

None of these flaws, however, hinders the book in delivering its message(s). Tocqueville had a message to send France and the world: The world we live in is a new one, not to be judged or navigated with the ideas of the past. The ancient world and its aristocracy are gone, never to return. "We must not try to make ourselves like our fathers but do our best to achieve the kind of grandeur and happiness that is appropriate to us." Democracy is inevitable, "but it is within [our] power to decide whether equality will lead . . . into servitude or liberty, enlightenment or barbarism, prosperity or misery." Freedom and democracy can be combined. The Americans have done so. It is neither necessary nor possible nor altogether desirable to copy the exact methods the Americans have used.

> But I do believe that if we do not manage to gradually introduce democratic institutions among us and ultimately to establish those institutions on a firm footing; and if we forsake the idea of instilling in all our citizens ideas and feelings that will first prepare them for liberty and then enable them to make use of it; then there will be no independence for anyone – not for the bourgeois or the noble, nor for the poor man or the rich man – but only equal tyranny for all. (364)

For Tocqueville, there is always a choice for human beings to make, and it is always the same choice – whether or not they wish to be free (834).

Democracy in America is a primer in how to make that choice wisely, amidst all the dangers of a democratic world. The battle for freedom can be won. America demonstrates this universal truth. "Let us therefore face the future with the salutary fear that keeps us vigilant and ready for battle, and not with the spineless and idle terror that afflicts and saps the heart" (830).

Democracy in America has, on balance, a happy ending. Tocqueville leaves behind a democratic and free America with the hope that America will remain so and the world will become so. The rest of his books, however, concern democracy in France, and as time went on Tocqueville became more and more pessimistic about the possibility of French freedom.

4

Democracy and Freedom in France

In 1848, revolution broke out (again) in France. The July Monarchy was overthrown, and the short-lived Second Republic (1848–51) took its place. Tocqueville's response can be found in his *Recollections*, a memoir written in 1850, intended for posthumous publication. In certain respects, the book is very different from anything else Tocqueville ever wrote. It discusses personalities, it paints lively vignettes, it is more concerned with individuals than with general ideas. The broad generalizations of *Democracy in America* and *The Old Regime and the Revolution* are largely missing. But the book has its own significance for a reader trying to understand Tocqueville's thought. Three points stand out: 1) Tocqueville's rejection of determinism. 2) Tocqueville's dislike of the bourgeoisie. 3) Tocqueville's growing pessimism about the future of freedom in France.

The first point is best made in Tocqueville's own words: "For my part, I hate all those absolute systems that make all the events of history depend on great first causes linked together by the chain of fate and thus succeed, so to speak, in banishing men from the history of the human race. Their boasted breadth seems to me narrow, and their mathematical exactness false" (*Reader*, 2002, 239).[1] In accord with this rejection of determinism, Tocqueville's *Recollections* analyze the causes of the Revolution of

---

[1] The point is already made in volume 2 of *Democracy* (2004, 570). For many years this quotation was read as Tocqueville's reply to Marx (whom he never read, and probably never heard of). More importantly, it is a warning to readers

1848 as a mixture of long-term, short-term and purely accidental developments. Tocqueville would later follow the same procedure in analyzing the French Revolution.

As for Tocqueville's dislike of the bourgeoisie, it can be found in *Democracy* and *The Old Regime* too. However, it is strongly emphasized in the *Recollections*. Tocqueville uses "bourgeois" and its variations essentially as a synonym for "middle class(es)," but in the early-nineteenth-century French context this referred to a relatively smaller and wealthier group of people than it would today. Tocqueville was furious at the bourgeoisie for mismanaging the July Monarchy and allowing another revolution. In the *Recollections*, "selfish," "greedy," "mediocre" and their variants are repeatedly used to describe the French middle class. But no matter how much he despised the bourgeoisie and the petty politics of the July Monarchy, he was a firm opponent of revolution in France, and no friend of the revolution of 1848. "I knew that, while one great revolution may be able to found a nation's liberty, several revolutions on top of each other [1789–1799, 1815, 1830, then 1848] make the enjoyment of an orderly liberty impossible there for a long time" (*Reader*, 2002, 242).

The Second Republic, with its see-sawing revolutions, counter-revolutions and finally Napoleon III's coup d'état deepened Tocqueville's pessimism about France, already visible by 1840. The threats to freedom that Tocqueville had described in America were present in democratic France, too, but the remedies the Americans had found seemed to be beyond the French grasp. In order to understand why democracy in France was harder to reconcile with freedom than democracy in America, Tocqueville turned to the history of the French Revolution. In 1856 he published *The Old Regime and the Revolution*, intended to be the first of two volumes on the subject.

---

of *Democracy* and *The Old Regime* not to take any prophecy about human affairs, even Tocqueville's, as a law of nature.

The French Revolution was not a new subject for Tocqueville. In 1836 he had published an essay about it in an English journal, at the request of its editor, his friend John Stuart Mill. The essay on "The Social and Political Condition of France before the Revolution" is important in its own right, and anticipated several of the themes of his later work, including the pre-Revolutionary rise of the centralized state, and the centuries-long growth of social equality. But *The Old Regime and the Revolution* is a masterpiece, a continuation on another continent of the story Tocqueville had told in America, the story of democracy and freedom.

Just as *Democracy in America* is not a conventional narrative account of the United States, so *The Old Regime* is not a conventional history. "This book is not a history of the French Revolution, whose story has been too brilliantly told for me to imagine retelling it. It is a study of the Revolution" (*Old Regime*, 1998a, 83). The methods of study are largely the same in the two books, with one notable exception, and so are the fundamental problems, although they sometimes take on new names because of different circumstances and Tocqueville's continued reflections on his essential questions.

When writing *The Old Regime*, Tocqueville still proceeded when he could by interviews, just as in *Democracy in America*. But since many of the people he would have liked to talk to were dead, Tocqueville was forced to develop a new method of interrogation: he went to the archives. He spent many months acting much like a twenty-first-century historian, taking notes on old papers. He also became a devoted reader of memoirs by participants in the Revolution.

The themes of his research would often be familiar to readers of *Democracy* – the essential Tocqueville did not change. In *The Old Regime* Tocqueville is still preoccupied with the effects of centralization, and contrasts its history in France with its history elsewhere. Other concerns of *Democracy in America* reappear in *The Old Regime*, although sometimes in altered guise. For example, the concept of individualism is transformed: Rather than emphasizing the threat posed to freedom by the individualism and materialism of isolated persons, *The Old Regime* portrays the collective individualism and isolation of classes. Instead of talking about how religion supports freedom, *The Old Regime* analyzes why in France freedom and religion were perceived as mortal enemies. Tocqueville continues to examine the relationship between democracy and freedom, but in the French context the relationship becomes largely negative. France is intensely democratic, always devoted to equality, but only occasionally interested in freedom.

This conclusion was devastating to Tocqueville. Finding an explanation for it, and ideally a way to reverse it, is at the heart of his enterprise in *The Old Regime*. Tocqueville never pretended to be interested in the past for its own sake: "I admit that in studying our old society in all its aspects, I have never entirely lost sight of our modern society." Tocqueville's commitments are on more or less continuous display in *The Old Regime*. His friend Gustave de Beaumont, consulted about the book's title, suggested that "what would best characterize the book's spirit and the general course of your ideas would be *Democracy and Freedom in France* . . ." Freedom is always on Tocqueville's mind. In *The Old Regime* French history is its setting, as a voyage to America had once been (*OR*, 1998a, 86; *OC*, 1967c, 373).

But neither freedom, nor France, nor democracy could be understood by an historian who only looked at a single country, in Tocqueville's view. The comparative method is at the heart of *The Old Regime*, just as it had been in *Democracy*. As Tocqueville put it in a chapter on "How Almost All of Europe Had Come to Have Identical Institutions and How These Institutions Fell into Ruin Everywhere," "whoever has seen and studied only France will never understand anything about the French Revolution." Tocqueville was firmly attached to the comparative methods he had first used in *Democracy in America*. Democracy was the subject, and France was a case study. At the very end of *The Old Regime*, however, Tocqueville wavered in this conclusion: "Without the reasons which I have given, the French would never have made the Revolution; but it must be recognized that all these reasons together would not succeed in explaining such a revolution anywhere else but in France." Tocqueville's rejection of determinism led him to a style of explanation that refused to choose between the general and the particular, and insisted on the importance of both (*OR*, 1998a, 247).

The methods of *Democracy*, suitably altered for a historical subject, thus produced *The Old Regime*. The work is divided into a brief preface and three books. The preface is largely a statement of Tocqueville's essential problem – how to reconcile democracy and freedom. He cites *Democracy*, and restates his credo that "liberty alone can effectively combat the natural vices of these kinds of societies" (*OR*, 1998a, 88). Book one, while short, makes a series of powerful arguments challenging the conventional wisdom about the meaning of the French Revolution. The French Revolution was not some vast anarchic uprising. Its goal "Was not, as has been thought, to destroy religion and weaken the state." If it was a political revolution that acted like a religious revolution, this was only because the Church had become a political and social institution, not because the Revolution was fundamentally hostile to religion. The Revolution took place in France, but it was the culmination of a movement taking place throughout European society. It broke out suddenly, but it was the fruit of historical developments that had begun centuries before. In sum, the Revolution was a social and political movement whose purpose was to destroy the rotting fabric of aristocratic society in Europe.

But why did this Revolution, which was essentially a European, or even, eventually, a universal phenomenon, "break out in France rather than somewhere else?" And "Why did it have certain characteristics [in France] which did not appear anywhere else, or did so only partially?" (107). To answer these questions, and to study the French Revolution proper, Tocqueville turns to the peculiarities of French history. Old-regime France was a place where people who had become basically the same had to live under laws and institutions that treated them as though they were different. Books two and three explain how France had become such a democratic society, and describe its struggles to emerge from a constricting shell of outgrown aristocratic institutions and attitudes. Here again Tocqueville returns to themes and problems seen in *Democracy in America*. Book two is largely devoted to French centralization and its effects. His argument that "Administrative Centralization Is an Institution of the Old Regime, and Not the Work of Either the Revolution or the Empire, as Is Said," while not entirely original, shocked many readers (118). At the time it was published, and for many readers since, the most striking part of *The Old Regime* is its denial that either the revolutionaries or Napoleon, the usual suspects, were the architects of the centralized French state. This is the so-called continuity thesis: French centralization was a centuries-long process that had been largely completed before the Revolution. This argument is a prime reason *The Old Regime and the Revolution* mostly discusses the old regime, that is, the last two centuries of the French monarchy.

In *Democracy in America*, Tocqueville described how a decentralized system of administration and local government, combined with local elections and a strong judiciary system, helped Americans preserve their freedom. In *The Old Regime*, Tocqueville describes the opposite: how a centralized royal administration destroyed or subverted local freedoms, eliminated local elections and emasculated the judiciary. In doing so, the monarchy leveled society, encouraged democracy and destroyed the power of the aristocracy. Book two's description of French centralization is as broad-ranging as *Democracy in America*'s description of American decentralization. In his account of the old regime Tocqueville discusses government paternalism, the creation of administrative courts and a centralized bureaucracy, and the way in which Paris gained ascendancy over the rest of the kingdom. Tocqueville explicitly and implicitly contrasts centralization in France to decentralization in America and England. For example, he compares the rural village of France to the New England township that was, for Tocqueville, the archetype of American local government. He finds remarkable similarities, derived from a common medieval past – New England's medieval past was old England. But the English township, transferred to New England, had been liberated from state control and blossomed. The French village had been "enclosed in the hand of the state." The result? "They resembled each other, in a word, as much as the living could resemble the dead" (*OR*, 1998a, 129). Freedom had flourished in decentralized America. It had been smothered in centralized France.

The monarchy sought to eliminate freedom, because freedom limited its authority. In Tocqueville's account the old regime divided the French into classes, cut them off from one another, made it difficult or pointless for them to act in common and pursued a consistent strategy of "divide and conquer." The strategy worked, for a time. Unfortunately, its effects outlasted the old regime, and made it near-impossible for the French to establish a free and stable government after the old regime ended. The class divisions fostered by the monarchy endured past its death. Its destruction of political freedom and local institutions resulted in a universal lack of political experience that hampered France long past 1789.

How did the old regime divide the French from one another while centralizing power? The tax system is Tocqueville's great example. By granting the nobility, the clergy and even many towns' special tax exemptions, the monarchy separated them from the rest of society. "Although inequality of taxation was established throughout the European continent, there were very few countries where it had become as visible and as constantly felt as in France." The result was a society in which every class and group was isolated from one another, even though they were becoming increasingly similar.

Our ancestors lacked the word "individualism," which we have created for our own use, because in their era there were, in fact, no individuals who did not belong to a group and who could consider themselves absolutely alone; but each one of the thousand little groups of which society was composed thought only of itself. This was, if one can use the word thus, a kind of collective individualism, which prepared people for the real individualism with which we are familiar. (156, 161–62)[2]

The democratic paradox in this seemingly undemocratic situation was that beneath all the distinctions of rank and privilege and taxation with which the old regime abounded, people had become more and more similar to one another. "France was the Country Where People had Become Most Alike," reads another of Tocqueville's chapter titles. Why? Because the nobles, while preserving their privileges, had lost their power and much of their wealth, the former to the king, the latter to the bourgeoisie. "Everyone above the masses resembled one another; they had the same ideas, the same habits, the same tastes, . . . read the same books, spoke the same language." Beneath the surface, France had become a democracy. The nobility had ceased to be an aristocracy, and become a mere caste. Tocqueville defines an aristocracy as "a group of citizens who govern," whereas a caste is defined by birth alone. As the monarchy took away the nobility's power to govern, and as the bourgeoisie rose in wealth and education and became more and more similar to the nobles in everything except pedigree, the nobility became merely a caste, a caste that attracted envy, jealousy, and finally hatred (149, 152).

How did this happen? Why was there no successful resistance to the kings' centralizing strategy? These are the crucial questions discussed in the chapter "How the Destruction of Political Liberty and the Division of Classes Caused Almost all the Ills of Which the Old Regime Perished" (163). From Tocqueville's

---

[2] However, one important difference between the collective individualism of the eighteenth century and later forms of democratic individualism is that in the old regime people "hardly knew that kind of passion for material well-being which is the mother of servitude . . ." (178). Here Tocqueville distinguished aristocratic France from middle-class America, to the advantage of the former.

perspective, it is poetic justice that the regime that centralized France perished in part because of centralization, and that those who destroyed French freedom were themselves destroyed.

The decline of French freedom, as Tocqueville tells the story, dates from the fourteenth or fifteenth century. In the Middle Ages, the nobles and the Third Estate would cooperate to preserve their freedoms against the monarchy. As the monarchy concentrated power in its hands after the Hundred Years' War with England, the nobles acquired more privileges but became increasingly isolated. Nobles and commoners no longer worked together. The Estates General, the assembly that represented the realm, met less and less frequently. Its last meeting before 1789 took place in 1614.

> As the general freedoms finally succumbed, pulling down local liberties in their ruin, the bourgeois and the noble no longer had contact with one another in public life . . . Every day they were more independent of each other, but also more estranged from one another. In the eighteenth century . . . The two classes were no longer merely rivals, they were enemies. (155)

Who killed freedom in France? The leading villains of Tocqueville's story are the kings and their ministers, the great architects of centralization. Louis XI, Richelieu and Louis XIV all merit mention, but it is the French monarchy as an institution that really bears the blame. The nobility, and the clergy and bourgeoisie are denounced as all-too-willing accomplices to freedom's murder. The only group in French society that gets off lightly in Tocqueville's account is the peasantry, who had no power to resist. Tocqueville's chapter on "How, Despite the Progress of Civilization, the Condition of the French Peasant Was Sometimes Worse in the Eighteenth Century Than it Had Been in the Thirteenth" is full of sympathy. But the peasants (and the urban poor) are by no means heroes in Tocqueville's account. They "could not avoid the yoke of false ideas, of vicious habits, of bad inclinations which their masters had given [them] . . ." In the end, the mass of the French people was left "as incapable of governing itself as its teachers had been of governing it." Tocqueville's pessimism could not be more marked. There is no social group left to be freedom's champion (180, 192).

The slow destruction of French freedom during the old regime turned out to be a lasting recipe for instability. The kind of freedom that remained, tucked away in nooks and crannies, is discussed in "Of the Kind of Freedom That Existed under the Old Regime and Its Influence on the Revolution" (171). While it was useful to revolutionaries, it was not of a sort to promote a stable, free government. The French had become ripe for a government that combined equality with centralized despotism – the kind they received so often after 1789.

Book two of *The Old Regime* is largely a discussion of the Revolution's long-term causes. French society had been prepared for revolution, and for democratic despotism, by its centralized political and administrative structure, by its collective individualism and by the lack of practical political experience that resulted from these things. In book three, Tocqueville leaves "the long-term and general facts which prepared the great Revolution . . . to come to the particular and more recent facts which finally determined its place, its birth, and its character" (195). From centuries, the time-scale narrows to the decades before 1789. Tocqueville discusses several factors, including how reforms, attempted reforms and even France's economic prosperity contributed to the Revolution. All these medium-term causes, however, were strongly influenced by the cause he discusses in chapter one of book three: the language and ideas of the French Enlightenment.

This chapter is full of words Tocqueville chooses to avoid, chief among them being "Enlightenment" itself, never used. Many conservatives were only too happy to blame all the evils of the Revolution on Rousseau and Voltaire, or the ideas of Enlightenment in general. This was not Tocqueville's perspective. As he wrote Gustave de Beaumont: "I did not want to criticize the ideas of the 18th century or, at least, the correct, reasonable, applicable portion of those ideas, which, after all, are my own." More broadly, Tocqueville did not write about the "Enlightenment" because he was not interested in analyzing ideas as such. It is the social and political context that gives ideas their meaning in his account. Many of the revolutionaries' ideas were old, and only in the circumstances of late-eighteenth-century France did they became popular and important. "Voltaire's ideas had long been abroad in the world; but Voltaire himself, in fact, could hardly have reigned anywhere but in the eighteenth century and in France" (*SL*, 1985, 330; *OR*, 1998a, 204).

Tocqueville also avoids talking about the "tyranny of the majority," with somewhat more excuse, since the tyranny over public opinion that he describes in this chapter is not, originally, exercised by the majority, although it comes to be a tyrannical form of majority opinion. In late-eighteenth-century France it was possible for a single set of ideas to rule, because people were basically similar. Whose ideas? Because the nobility had ceased to be an aristocracy, the ideas that ruled eighteenth-century France were not theirs. Alternatively, the leading ideas might have come from the monarchy or the Church, but the monarchy, like the Church, was inextricably tied to all the privileges and inequalities in French society, despite its leveling role. Instead, the new egalitarian ideas, and the new words that were on everyone's lips came from a new source, absent from book two of *The Old Regime*, and absent from *Democracy in America* as well. Book three, chapter one, is devoted to "How Around the Middle of the Eighteenth Century Intellectuals Became the Country's Leading Politicians, and the Effects Which Resulted from This" (*OR*, 1998a, 195).

The political importance of intellectuals and their ideas was, according to Tocqueville, new and unique to France. Although the writers differed from one another enormously, they shared certain crucial traits. While they were almost never directly involved in politics, they all wrote about it. Still more important, in a crucial respect they all wrote the same thing: "They all think that it would be good to substitute basic and simple principles, derived from reason and natural law, for the complicated and traditional customs which ruled the society of their times" (196). Nothing could be more democratic than this, nor more revolutionary, but no one realized its revolutionary implications until much later.

These "men of letters" exercised enormous influence, largely because no one, themselves included, had any real political experience. For Tocqueville, real politics can only take place if there is political freedom. Since the government had confiscated French freedom, no one, not even the government, had any real experience of practical politics. "There is nothing, in fact, but the play of free institutions which can really teach politicians this principal part of their art." As a result, the writers' ideas were not reined in by reality. By contrast, the same ideas, when published by English authors in a free country, fell on deaf ears, or provoked opposition. In France, logic ruled unchecked by facts (200).

In Tocqueville's account, circumstances are the deciding factor in the role intellectuals and their ideas played in the Revolution. Tocqueville is not attacking intellectuals, nor even the ideas of the Enlightenment. He is attacking their operation in a political and social vacuum, in which intellectuals usurped powers that ought to have been divided among the rest of society. The result of this usurpation by the intellectuals was that their abstract and logical language spread everywhere. The nobles adopted it. So did royal edicts, which spoke of natural law and the rights of men. Even peasants, "in their requests, called their neighbors their fellow citizens; . . . the parish priest, the minister of the altars; God, the Supreme Being. To become mediocre men of letters, all they had to do was learn how to spell" (202). The intellectuals' language became the language of the majority, and exercised all the influence over the coming and course of the Revolution that one would expect in a democratic society.[3] Thus:

---

[3] This point of Tocqueville's is the heart of François Furet's and Keith Baker's argument for the crucial role of language in the French Revolution.

In the absence of any other directors, in the midst of the profound practical ignorance in which they lived, the whole nation ended up adopting the instincts, the attitudes, the tastes, and even the eccentricities of those who write, with the result that when the nation finally had to act, it brought all the habits of literature into politics.

When we study the history of our Revolution, we see that it was carried out in precisely the same spirit in which so many abstract books on government are written. The same attraction for general theories, for complete systems of legislation and exact symmetry of laws; the same contempt for existing facts . . . (201)[4]

This contributed greatly to making the French Revolution the unprecedented event it was: "This situation, so new to history, in which the entire political education of a great nation was shaped by men of letters, was perhaps what contributed most to giving the French Revolution its particular spirit, and made it lead to what we see today" (201). The writers, with their simple principles based on reason and logic, preferred radical change to moderation, and revolution to reform.

The intellectuals also contributed a good deal to the hostility between the Revolution and religion, one of the most important ways in which democracy in France and democracy in America differed. Writers spread irreligion in France with the same zeal with which they spread other rational reforms. They experienced just enough retaliation from the established Church to irritate them. Nowhere else in Europe were their ideas as successful as in France. Anti-religious writing made no headway

---

[4] It is in this context that Tocqueville gives, in a nutshell, his explanation of the Terror that would strike France in 1793: "The contrast between benign theories and violent acts which is one of the French Revolution's strangest characteristics, will not surprise anyone who notes that that revolution had been prepared by the most civilized classes of the nation, and carried out by the most coarse and ignorant" (243) – as has been true many times since.

in England, although it appeared there, Tocqueville thought, even before France. The English knew that irreligion was dangerous to society. The French, ignorant from lack of freedom, did not. In *The Old Regime*, Tocqueville argues that "to believe that democratic societies are naturally hostile to religion is to commit a great mistake: nothing in Christianity, nothing even in Catholicism, is absolutely contrary to the spirit of democratic societies, and many things are very favorable." Why then did the Revolution turn churches into warehouses, and persecute priests? "The priests were not hated because they claimed to regulate the affairs of the other world, but because they were landowners, lords, tithe collectors, and administrators in this one." The Catholic Church had become so deeply involved in the social and political structure of the old regime that any attack on the old regime was inevitably an attack on the Church. The implication was that Church and State were better off separated, as they were in America (205).

The Revolution's hostility to the Church, however, led Tocqueville's contemporaries to what he saw as the false conclusion that the Revolution, democracy and freedom were all fundamentally anti-religious phenomena. Tocqueville had fought this attitude in *Democracy in America*, pointing out how in America freedom and religion were considered natural allies. In *The Old Regime*, he attempted to explain how they had become natural enemies in France. The rivalry between writers and priests for influence over the French mind had far-reaching consequences that were, in the long run, as dangerous for secular government as for the Church.

But even more striking to Tocqueville than hostility to religion was the fervor with which irreligion was embraced. Hatred for one particular religion was nothing new in European history. New was the fervent desire to have no religion at all.

Established religions had been attacked in other times and places, but the feeling against them had always been inspired by new religions . . . In France, Christianity was attacked with a kind of fury, without even an attempt to put another religion in its place. Many worked constantly and ardently to sever souls from the faith that had filled them, leaving them empty. (203)

Human souls naturally abhor a vacuum, and the religious vacuum left by the discredit of Christianity was no exception. Catholicism was replaced by philosophical doctrines that called on the French

> to transform society and regenerate our species. These feelings and passions had become a kind of new religion for them, which, producing some of the great effects which we have seen religions produce, tore them away from individual [and collective] egoism, encouraged them to heroism and devotion, and often made them seem insensible to all the petty goods which we possess. (208)

Like Christianity and Islam, like no other previous political movement, the French Revolution was universal in its claims. The Rights of Man proclaimed by the revolutionaries respected no national boundaries, and revolutionaries flocked to one another's aid regardless of what language they spoke, because all spoke the same, universal language of rights. "The French Revolution operated, with respect to this world, in precisely the same manner that religious revolutions have acted with respect to the other world. It considered the citizen in an abstract manner, outside of any particular society, the same way that religion considers man in general, independently of time and place" (100).

The democratic society coming into being throughout Europe made this possible. The new revolutionary religion, or "revolutionary disease," as Tocqueville also called it, had a worldwide vocation because democracy was becoming the social state worldwide. Once democracy had arrived, there was no turning back. The revolutionary era, the era of international political movements, had begun. Soon it would spread from Europe to the rest of the world. As Tocqueville wrote in a note, "the French Revolution has left in the world a spirit of uneasiness and anarchy which seems eternal . . . for sixty years [from 1789 until the time of writing] there has continued to be a great revolutionary school open in some part of the world, where all violent, insubordinate, or perverse minds go to train and instruct themselves". He could have been speaking of the Soviet Union, or Castro's Cuba, or the latest center of Jihad. As indeed he prophesied: "one must not think that these new beings were the isolated or ephemeral creations of a moment, destined to pass with it; they have since formed a race which has perpetuated itself, and spread among all civilized parts of the earth. . . . We found them in the world when we were born; they are still with us" (209, 323).

France in the late eighteenth century was a powder keg primed to explode. Once the explosion took place, there was nothing to limit it. Ideas, mores and institutions were all such as to make radical change likely. Although Tocqueville would have liked to believe that a reformed monarchy, rather than a Revolution, was possible (his appendix on the province of Languedoc describes his vision), he himself doubted it.

In itself, the Revolution was not necessarily a bad thing from Tocqueville's perspective. He favored democratic society. He described the old regime as detestable, even though in doing so he risked condemnation from many of his own class and family. He always described himself as a supporter of "1789," that is, of the beginning of the French Revolution. The problem was that France had been prepared for democracy and for Revolution, but not for freedom. The monarchy had strengthened the state, but had weakened or destroyed free institutions. In America, history, mores and institutions had all been prepared for freedom long before the thirteen colonies claimed their independence. In France, more than a Revolution was required to establish a free country.

The first requirement for freedom, Tocqueville tells us, is simple: it is to want to be free. In democratic societies, everyone feels a strong desire for equality, but freedom is another matter. If in *Democracy in America* the optimistic Tocqueville thought that the desire for freedom was natural to human beings, in *The Old Regime* he is less certain. In his notes he wrote: "But who gives men the desire for freedom, if they have not known it or have lost it? . . . Who will make them love it for itself, if this love is not naturally in their heart? . . . Interest will never be visible enough and permanent enough to keep the love of liberty in men's hearts, if desire does not keep it there." Tocqueville then returns to his original position, but with a different emphasis: Freedom is "A desire which is found, it is true, in all men, but which only holds first place in the hearts of a small number." Tocqueville had come a long way from putting his hope in self-interest properly understood in *Democracy* (*OR*, 1998a, 396–97).

However, for a short time, in the decades leading up to the Revolution, the French decided that they were not satisfied with being equal, they also wanted to be free. In this period France harbored two passions. One, for equality, was old and well-rooted.

> The other passion, more recent and less well-rooted, brought them to want to live, not only equal, but free. Toward the end of the old regime these two passions are equally sincere and seem equally lively. At the start of the Revolution they meet; they mix and join for a moment and then, . . . finally inflame the whole heart of France at once. This is '89 . . .

The year 1789 and the year or two before it is the high point of the Revolution for Tocqueville. Before illness and death interrupted his work on volume two of *The Old Regime*, this is the period he concentrated on, because this was the most exciting, vital and potentially fruitful portion of the Revolution. Instead of focusing on decades, as book three of *The Old Regime* does, the first book of volume two focuses on a couple of years, 1787 and 1788. Later books would have narrowed the focus to months or even days, as Tocqueville mulled over just when the Revolution had turned away from freedom. Was it as late as October 1789, when the king and the National Assembly were forced to move from Versailles to Paris by the Paris mob? Or was it when the Bastille fell in July, or was the situation already doomed once the Estates General had met in May and the recalcitrance of the privileged order and the incompetence of the royal government emerged beyond doubt? Tocqueville hesitated over these dates and the question of when things turned definitively downhill. But the high point is clear. It is the moment in April 1789 when the Estates General of France were finally about to meet and reclaim their rights after an interval of 165 years: "I do not believe that at any moment in history, at any place on earth, a similar multitude of men has ever been seen so sincerely impassioned for the public good, so truly forgetful of their interests, so determined . . . This first spectacle was short, but it had incomparable beauty. It will never depart from human memory" (68, 244).

Whenever the turning point was, the turn took place, and France turned away from freedom. Instead of freedom uniting the French, class passions and class struggles, much more emphasized in volume two of *The Old Regime* than in volume one, helped tear them apart. The old regime's effects, results of the monarchy's attempts to separate the classes so as to better rule them, lingered on after its violent death. Napoleon was a natural resting point for a democratic revolution that had lost interest in freedom. We have two draft chapters about France in 1799, just before Napoleon took power, which portray an exhausted nation looking for a ruler, ready to give up anything in exchange, provided it could retain its equality. Freedom had become the least of its concerns.[5]

The decades after 1799 showed that France was not content even with a despot, however. The old regime had created a France doomed to alternate between democratic anarchy and democratic despotism. As Tocqueville put it in another note,

---

[5] See *The Old Regime* (2001b), and on the theme of class struggle in particular, Kahan (1985).

"France is neither Bourbon, nor liberal, but revolutionary and servile" (415). In *Democracy in America* Tocqueville described how freedom could be preserved in a democratic society. In *The Old Regime*, he described how it could be lost. Tocqueville remained pessimistic about the prospects for freedom in France until his death in 1859, three years after its publication.

5

Democracy and Freedom Elsewhere

The nineteenth century was the age of colonialism. Many European powers, France included, created great empires during this period. Not coincidentally, perhaps, the nineteenth century also saw the development of what is sometimes called "scientific racism," whose invention is often attributed to Tocqueville's private secretary during his period as foreign minister, Arthur de Gobineau. Tocqueville's correspondence with Gobineau about racism, his writings and speeches on the French conquest and colonization of Algeria and his writings on the British conquest of India give us insight into how he projected his concerns for France and for freedom onto the canvas of imperialism.

Tocqueville was not a racist. This was more unusual among nineteenth-century European writers on social and political questions than one would like to think. Even some of the most liberal minds of the day were occasionally guilty of casual anti-Semitic or anti-Black or anti-Asian remarks. Not Tocqueville.

But this fact should not obscure Tocqueville's support for European and especially French colonialism. Tocqueville was a nationalist, and in some respects an extreme nationalist. In 1840 he shocked John Stuart Mill by being willing to run the risk of war between France and England over disputes in the Middle East, rather than risk diminishing France's national pride. Mill should not have been shocked. In *Democracy in America*, which Mill had reviewed, Tocqueville wrote that

I do not wish to speak ill of war. War almost always enlarges the thought and ennobles the heart of a people. There are cases

in which war alone can halt the excessive development of
certain penchants to which equality naturally gives rise, and in
which it must be considered a necessary corrective to certain deep-
seated afflictions of democratic societies; (*Democracy*, 2004, 765).

For Tocqueville, patriotism and even war could serve to combat
individualism (*OC*, 1954, 330).

However, Tocqueville's nationalism sometimes conflicted with
other values he held dear. This is particularly evident in his
writings about Algeria and India, where he could never arrive at
a lasting synthesis. If Tocqueville's views on race will be satisfac-
tory to most twenty-first-century readers, his views on colonialism evoke a much wider range of reactions, partly because they
are not nearly so consistent.

Anyone familiar with Tocqueville's rejection of all forms of
determinism, and his determination to maintain human freedom, will not be surprised at his rejection of racism, although
Gobineau was. Gobineau published the racist classic, *Essay on the
Inequality of Human Races*, in 1853. In it he vaunted the superiority of the "Aryan race" over all others, and proclaimed the
inevitable decline of nations, such as the French, whose Aryan
essence had been mingled with lesser breeds. He sent a copy to
Tocqueville, his former boss. Over the next several years they
engaged in an extended discussion by correspondence of
Gobineau's theories, although Tocqueville increasingly tried to
change the subject.

From the very beginning, Tocqueville categorically rejected
Gobineau's main ideas. "Your basic idea," Tocqueville wrote
when Gobineau sent him the work, "seems to me to belong to the
family of materialist theories, and even to be one of the most
dangerous of them, since it is fatalism applied to, not merely
the individual, but to these collections of individuals called
races . . ." When Gobineau was surprised by the hostile response,
Tocqueville rejected his theory again, on the grounds that it was
harmful to humanity: "Do you not see that your doctrine
brings out naturally all the evils that permanent inequality

creates – pride, violence, the contempt of fellow men, tyranny, and abjectness in all its forms?" When Gobineau objected that even if his theory might have harmful effects, this did not make it less true, Tocqueville responded that "I did not become sufficiently German in studying the German language for the novelty or philosophical merit of an idea to make me forget the moral or political effect that it can produce." Tocqueville never let anything sway him from his attachment to freedom. But this is not to say that he would otherwise have found Gobineau's theories convincing. Pushed to the wall by a Gobineau desperate for approbation, Tocqueville argued that Gobineau's theories led to "a very great contraction, if not a complete abolition, of human liberty. Well, I confess to you that after having read you, as well as before, I remain situated at the opposite extreme of those doctrines. I believe them to be very probably wrong and very certainly pernicious." When, years later, Gobineau again importuned Tocqueville, he cited scripture in reply: "What is more clear in Genesis than the unity of humankind and the emergence of all men from the same man? And as for the spirit of Christianity, is not its distinctive trait having wanted to abolish all distinctions of race . . . and making only one human species, all of whose members were equally capable of perfecting themselves and of becoming alike?" Finally Tocqueville asked Gobineau not to discuss his political theories with him anymore (*OC,* 1959, 199; *SL,* 1985, 298–99, 303, 343).

It is in the light of his absolute rejection of racism that Tocqueville's comments on Blacks and native Americans must be understood. Tocqueville's views about race relations between Blacks and Whites in the United States have already been discussed. It bears repeating, however, that his fundamental presupposition was the essential equality of Blacks and Whites and the absolute moral evil of slavery. His views of the native Americans demonstrate the way in which contact with American reality changed his preconceptions, while reaffirming his essential commitment to human equality. When he arrived in the United States, he was full of Romantic notions about the noble and graceful savages who roamed the American woods of his imagination. He was terribly disappointed when he saw his first Indians, a group of the formerly feared Iroquois, begging and drinking outside a town in northern New York. In his notebooks he described the Indians of New York as a "population brutalized by our wines and our liquors. More horrible than the equally brutalized peoples of Europe" (Pierson 224–25).

Nevertheless, this shock did not lead Tocqueville to regard the native Americans with contempt. In his view the native Americans had "surely demonstrated as much natural genius as the peoples of Europe . . ." If their situation had degraded, it was not hard to find the culprit. Tocqueville speaks of "European tyranny" and "oppression," and describes the destruction the Indians' way of life by European agricultural and hunting practices. Already at the time of his visit in 1831 the buffalo had disappeared from many Midwestern regions where they once flourished. In the East, their lands had been taken from them. In the West, their lands had been made incapable of supporting their way of life – and soon those too would be gone. Everywhere, they were constantly harassed. On his voyage down the Mississippi river, Tocqueville encountered a group of Choctaw Indians being forcibly relocated from Georgia to the West. "I watched them embark for the voyage across the great river, and the memory of that solemn spectacle will stay with me forever" (*Democracy*, 2004, 374, 385).

Tocqueville offered the native Americans his pity, but he could not offer them any hope: "I believe that the Indian race in North America is doomed, and I cannot help thinking that by the time Europeans have settled the Pacific coast, it will have ceased to exist." The Indians would either have been wiped out or forced to lose their identity through complete assimilation into European culture. Tocqueville thought that most would prefer the former alternative. "Only two avenues of salvation were open to the Indians of North America: war or civilization. In other words they had either to destroy the Europeans or to become their equals." The former was impossible from a very early date.

The later was impossible for the simple reason that "the Indians will never want to become civilized, or . . . by the time they do want to do so, it will be too late." Tocqueville regarded the Indians as too proud to give up a nomadic and independent life of hunting and farming (*Democracy*, 2004, 376, 377).[1]

But this did not lead Tocqueville to make convenient racial explanations of national character. Instead, Tocqueville compared the native Americans' attitudes to those of his own ancestors': "The Indian, in the depths of his sylvan misery, thus nurses the same ideas and the same opinions as the medieval nobleman in his fortified castle, and all he needs to end up resembling him is to become a conqueror." Tocqueville goes on to liken the behavior of the native Americans to that of the Germanic tribes described by Tacitus in the second century A.D., and concludes that "I cannot help thinking that the same cause produced the same effects in both hemispheres . . . In what we call Germanic institutions, therefore, I am tempted to see nothing other than barbarian habits, just as I am tempted to see the opinions of savages in what we call feudal ideas." What could be less racist than this equation of the native Americans with the supposed Germanic ancestors of the French nobility (*Democracy*, 2004, 379)?

Besides the rejection of racism, there is another important point made in the correspondence with Gobineau. Commentators on Tocqueville have often noted his growing pessimism. But Tocqueville at his most pessimistic puts limits on his pessimism. He was never resigned to inevitable human failure. If Tocqueville laments the nineteenth century in certain respects, its growing materialism, individualism, and so on, he also recognizes its virtues. As he tells a truly pessimistic Gobineau: "I am often annoyed with humanity. Who wouldn't be . . .? But not against

---

[1] Tocqueville was aware that some Indian tribes did practice agriculture, and discusses the Cherokees and the Choctaws in particular, but for various reasons he thinks their efforts to partly assimilate to European civilization are doomed. See *Democracy* (2004, 380–81, 383).

the century, which, after all, will count as one of the great centuries of history; the one in which man most subjected nature and completed the conquest of the globe" (*OC*, 1959, 229).

It is difficult to tell if the conquest of the globe Tocqueville had in mind was scientific or political. Shortly before the restored Bourbons finally lost power in 1830, France had conquered Algiers. During the July Monarchy, France extended its power over all Algeria and began European colonization. Looking back on this process in 1847, Tocqueville wrote to General Lamoricière, one of the military leaders of the campaign:

> From the moment when we committed that great *violence* of the conquest, I believe that we ought not to draw back from all the little violences which are absolutely necessary to consolidate it. But, in the interest of our establishment itself, it is very important to put on our side, as much as possible, in the eyes of the natives, the law, and if not the law, at least humanity and a certain consideration. (Jaume 408)

Combining humanity with violence was much like squaring the circle. Tocqueville never succeeded in it. But it was not for lack of trying. Tocqueville probably was more involved with Algerian affairs than with any other single issue during his parliamentary career under the July Monarchy, with the possible exception of antislavery. Even before then, he had been much concerned with Algeria. His friend and cousin Louis de Kergorlay was a member of the first military expedition to Algeria in 1830, and in 1833 he and Tocqueville seem to have briefly considered settling there. Tocqueville published two letters on Algeria in 1837, during his unsuccessful first campaign for the Chamber of Deputies. Afterwards, he made lengthy trips to Algeria in 1841 and 1846, and was a prominent and active participant in the assembly's debates on Algeria.

On most issues associated with Algeria, Tocqueville often hesitated and changed his mind. On one point, however, Tocqueville never wavered. Having conquered, France must remain master of Algeria. "In the eyes of the world, such an abandonment would be the clear indication of our decline . . . Any people that easily gives up what it has taken and chooses to retire peacefully to its original borders proclaims that its age of greatness is over." And yet, in the next paragraph of this unpublished essay of 1841, Tocqueville almost backtracks: "If France ever abandons Algeria, it is clear that she could do it only at a moment when she is seen undertaking great things in Europe, and not at a time such as our own, when she appears to be falling into the second rank and seems resigned to let the control of European affairs pass into other hands." Is Tocqueville really committed to French Algeria, or is it a question of circumstances? At any rate, there would be no point in leaving, for then Algeria would simply be taken over by another European power (*Writings*, 2001a, 59–60).

Tocqueville was attached to Algeria as a symbol of French power, almost of French virility. Although there were a handful of parliamentarians who wanted to withdraw from Algeria, Tocqueville was in agreement with the vast majority of French public opinion. Parliamentary debates about Algerian policy were heated because of disputes about means, not ends. Tocqueville himself was morally conflicted about everything that followed once the nationalist imperative of upholding French power and prestige was accepted. He wrote in 1841, after his first trip to Algeria: "For my part, I returned from Africa with the distressing notion that we are now fighting far more barbarously than the Arabs themselves. For the present it is on their side that one meets with civilization . . . It was certainly not worth taking the Turks' place in order to recreate that aspect of their rule that deserved the world's abhorrence." Yet after this astonishing admission, Tocqueville continued, "On the other hand, I have often heard men in France whom I respect, but with whom I do not agree, find it wrong that we burn harvests, that we empty silos, and finally that we seize unarmed men, women and children. These, in my view, are unfortunate necessities . . ." (25, 70).

Tocqueville was no less conflicted about what kind of relation France could have with the natives. His earliest writings on the subject were almost Utopian. In 1837 he hoped that eventually French and Arabs would one day form a "single people" in Algeria. But by 1846 he was proclaiming in assembly debate "that the idea of possessing Africa, of keeping Africa with the aid and support of the indigenous population – that idea, that dream of noble and generous hearts, is a chimera, at least for the present." Assimilation to French culture was another chimera. "It would undoubtedly be as dangerous as it would be useless to seek to suggest to them our mores, our ideas, our customs. It is not along the road of our European civilization that they must, for the present, be pushed . . ." The French and native peoples would remain separate (146).

Yet Tocqueville also attacked those who claimed that the only course of action was either to exterminate the natives or to push them entirely out of French territory:

> Let us not, in the middle of the nineteenth century, begin the history of the conquest of America over again, let us not imitate the bloody examples that the opinion of the human race has stigmatized. Let us bear in mind that we would be a thousand times less excusable than those who once had the misfortune of setting such examples; for we are less fanatical, and we have the principles and the enlightenment the French Revolution spread throughout the world. (142, 145–46)

What, then, was to be done? Tocqueville promoted decentralized administration, European colonization and for the native Arab and Berber-speaking populations, the creation of a community of interests with the French that would not eliminate hostile feelings, but dampen them. How? "Let us not force the indigenous peoples to come to our schools, but help them rebuild theirs, multiply the number of teachers, and create men of law and men of religion, which Muslim civilization cannot do without, any more than our own." Common interests could further be fostered by encouraging commerce, protecting Arab property beyond what was immediately necessary for colonization and by good government and the rule of law (142).

Tocqueville's conclusion in 1846 was weak, and he knew it. In attempting to use the remedies against despotism he had found in America in a colonial context, he was striking a false note, because his chief concern in Algeria was not freedom. Throughout his discussion of Algerian questions, freedom takes a backseat to national interest. Tocqueville was never willing to see freedom take a backseat to power in France itself. He repeatedly rejected this argument in a French context, whether made on behalf of Louis XIV or of Napoleon. Nothing could be sufficient compensation to the French for the loss of liberty. But when it came to Algerians, that was another matter. French national interest trumped foreigners' rights. But Tocqueville shrank from confronting the consequences of this conclusion – hence the twists and turns of his writing once the need to maintain French power in Algeria had been asserted. But what about when two foreign nations were concerned, Britain and India?

In 1841–43, shortly after completing *Democracy in America*, Tocqueville entertained the project of writing one or two articles about the British conquest of India, with Algeria in mind. What lessons for France might there be in Britain's success in ruling India? The project was abandoned, but not before Tocqueville had done a considerable amount of reading, and left many notes and drafts. Tocqueville returned to the subject of India again in 1857, when the Great Rebellion against British rule occurred. His English wife was deeply distressed, and Tocqueville became an avid reader of news on the subject, and corresponded about it with English friends.

From these writings it emerges that even when Tocqueville was a bystander, he was still a nationalist, and thought that others should be too – including Indians. He rejected the racist view that the Indians had failed to successfully resist the British because they were cowards by nature. Instead, he blamed their inability on history, religion and mores. Above all he blamed the caste system, which effectively destroyed the nation. In India, "there are a multitude of castes . . ., there is no nation . . ." and "in a country of castes, the idea of the fatherland, of nationality, disappears in a sense." Hinduism, in Tocqueville's eyes, had the fatal flaw of rejecting the idea that all human beings were fundamentally equal. This helped Hinduism acquire the merit of not inspiring religious fanaticism as long as it was not interfered with, since Hindus had no interest in proselytizing, or persecuting other religions. But it deprived Hinduism "of the one good one has a right to expect from even the worst religions. It never inspired the Indians with that pious fury which has led so many peoples to oppose a conquest when the conqueror professes a different faith than theirs and which has led them to save their nationality in wishing to honor their religion" (*OC*, 1962, 447–49, 537).

Alongside the caste system, Tocqueville held up for contempt India's princes. No modern Indian nationalist could be more scathing in his condemnation of Indian rulers' collaboration with the British than Tocqueville (by contrast, he had nothing but respect for Abd-el-Kader, the Algerian leader). Tocqueville repeatedly remarks on Indian princes' incompetence, childishness and refusal to unite against the English. The English task of conquest was an easy one. Any European nation could have conquered India in the eighteenth century, according to Tocqueville.

What interested Tocqueville most was not the easy conquest of India, although he was interested in why it was so easy. What interested him was how the English had managed to *keep* India, and for relatively little cost. This is where he thought France might find lessons for Algeria. However, the more he examined the government of the East India Company, the worse it seemed. Tocqueville was contemptuous of the legal system the English imposed on those parts of India they ruled directly. We can probably find the reason for Tocqueville's abandoning work on the project in the lack of lessons it seemed likely to provide for French colonization of Algeria.

This makes Tocqueville's return to the subject in 1857 all the more interesting. Tocqueville had withdrawn from public life in

1852, after Napoleon III took power, and had said almost nothing about Algeria in public or in correspondence since. In his correspondence about the Indian rebellion, he seems to take some very different positions than those he had taken about Algeria. Is the difference due to circumstances, or had Tocqueville changed his mind about colonization in general?

Not all his positions changed. In 1857, Tocqueville wanted the English to stay in India as much as he ever wanted the French to stay in Algeria. Indeed, their withdrawal would be "disastrous for the future of civilization and the progress of humanity." He did not blame the revolt on English oppression, but rather on the progress Indians had made in their ideas of government and administration under English influence (*OC*, 1954, 230).

Nevertheless, he does blame the English. Referring to previous work in 1841–43, he writes, "the thought still stays with me from this study that the English had not in a century done anything for the Indian populations that might have been expected from their enlightenment and their institutions." In contrast to his friend John Stuart Mill, who worked for the East India Company and did his best to preserve it, Tocqueville argued that "I would like to see the East India Company abolished . . . Only then will you attain the level of your task, which is not only to dominate India, but to civilize it." In this regard there are both similarities and differences with earlier positions. England, like France, has a "civilizing mission" to perform, although the encouragement for indigenous culture Tocqueville hoped to provide in Algeria is absent from his remarks about India (*SL*, 1985, 359–60).

On the other hand, in one respect Tocqueville's attitude to India is radically different from his attitude to Algeria: he completely rejects the desirability of introducing European settlers to India. "I confess that I consider such a remedy, if it could be applied, so dangerous that I would be tempted to return to the laws that prevented the purchase of lands in India." He goes on to argue that India can only be held "with the consent, at least tacit, of the Indians," a position he regarded as chimerical with regard to Algeria in 1846. Introducing English settlers would, he thinks, make that consent impossible. European settlement has created "more anger . . . than . . . any political oppression." Had the French experience in Algeria changed his mind about colonization, as opposed to conquest? Would the later Tocqueville have opposed French settlement in North Africa? We cannot tell for sure (*SL*, 1985, 363).

Tocqueville also criticized English racism in India. The English were far less likely to form a "single race" with the Indians than the French ever were with the Arabs of Algeria. Indeed, Tocqueville puts the root cause of the mutiny of much of the Indian army down to the combination of Indian soldiers with British officers, who nevertheless held aloof from them, thus arousing their resentment. The events in India were "the revolt of barbarism against pride." In the modern world, even in India, it seems, it is impossible to maintain a European aristocracy. To attempt it is only to encourage jealousy, hatred and, in the end, revolution (*SL*, 1985, 362–64).

Anticolonial revolutions, from Tocqueville's 1857 perspective, are likely to be successful. Discussing the Second Opium War (1857–58) between England and China, he wrote an English friend:

> to return to China. It seems to me that the relations between that country and Europe are changed, and dangerously changed. Till now, Europe has had to deal only with a Chinese government – the most wretched of governments. Now you will find opposed to you a people; and a people, however miserable and corrupt, is invincible on its own territory, if it be supported and impelled by common and violent passions. (Correspondence with Senior, 2004b, March 8, 1857)

Does this mean that Tocqueville foresaw that one day France would be defeated in Algeria, if the local population ever united against it? More broadly, was Tocqueville predicting that colonial independence was an unintended by-product of the European colonial enterprise itself since, as the Indian and Chinese examples showed, prolonged European domination could not help but improve the natives' desire and ability to unite against the colonial power (*Correspondence*, March 8, 1857, 2004b)?

As always for Tocqueville, democracy is inevitable, even, to some extent, in Hindu India. Freedom is another matter. Algerians and Indians and Chinese may be destined to national independence, but Tocqueville says nothing about European domination preparing them for freedom. Whatever the subject, Tocqueville's essential concerns remain the same: The future of France, the future of freedom, in a democratic world. But he is less concerned about freedom in some places than in others. Generous minds will prefer to think that this attitude would have changed had Tocqueville had the benefit of our historical experience.

6

Democracy, Freedom and Poverty

For Tocqueville, the problem of poverty never had the significance of democracy or freedom. Economic issues were never central to his values, and rarely to his analyses. Tocqueville's meager commentary on economics in his major works contributed after his death to his eclipse by Marx. However, the contemporary revival of interest in Tocqueville has renewed attention to his views on socioeconomic issues, and it has become clear that he devoted considerable attention to them. Tocqueville regarded economic problems, and particularly the problem of industrial poverty, as among the most important questions of his time. Examination of his writings reveals a sustained interest in the problem of poverty in modern society. In his view, the growing problem of industrial poverty was a corollary of the development of modern democratic society and posed a unique threat to freedom.

The average reader of Tocqueville may be forgiven for not noticing this, however. Economic and social questions do not much appear in the first volume of *Democracy in America*, except indirectly through the democratic obsession with making money. They appear only fleetingly in the second volume, and their role in *The Old Regime and the Revolution* is secondary and purely historical. If they play a larger role in the *Recollections*, this seems to be an accident related to the events of 1848. The problem of poverty is not central to these works because, in Tocqueville's view, it was not a life or death issue for France, or an immediate threat to freedom in democratic societies. He believed it might become such an issue however, which is why, throughout his career, he thought that "a more equal division of goods and rights in this world is the greatest object that those who direct human affairs can set themselves" (*OC*, 1983, 292).

Economic questions attracted Tocqueville's interest from the beginning of his adult life. When still a law student he read the work of the prominent liberal economist Jean-Baptiste Say. Tocqueville's attention was drawn to the problem of poverty by his voyage to England in 1833. At the time the English were engaged in a radical reform of the "Poor Law." The Poor Law Amendment Act of 1834 was intended to replace a system of financial relief that dated back to 1601 with one more suited, or so it was thought, to modern conditions. Tocqueville engaged in serious research on the reformed English Poor Law and its effects (Drolet 36–53, 95–114; Keslassy 43). He visited England again in 1835, and was shocked by the abject poverty he saw in industrial Manchester, then the center of the European textile industry. He also visited Birmingham, equally industrial but with a more prosperous working class, but feared that conditions there would soon change for the worse (*OC*, 1958, 73–74, 79–83).

If England taught Tocqueville to fear the effects of industrialization, his main concern, as always, was France, and his writings about poverty and economics were directed at France. In 1835 he produced his "First Memoir [Report] on Pauperism," for the Royal Academic Society of Cherbourg (Cherbourg was a port town not far from the village of Tocqueville). A "Second Memoir," never finished, was drafted in 1837 for the same society.

When we read the "Memoirs" today, they seem to be a curious blend of philosophy, economics and politics. Concern for economic *and* moral *and* political effects was typical of Tocqueville's attitude towards measures to relieve poverty. In a letter of 1834 he wrote that "while all the efforts of political economy [economics] in our day seem to me to be about material issues, I would like . . . to highlight the more immaterial side of this science . . . to include in it the ideas, the feelings of morality as elements of prosperity and happiness . . . to rehabilitate spiritualism . . ." This broad view was consistent with Tocqueville's essential concerns. Poverty mattered to Tocqueville primarily because of how it affected democratic societies' capacity for freedom. Tocqueville was also following in the footsteps of Adam Smith and Rousseau and other eighteenth-century theorists of "commercial society," rather than the developing Classical school of economic thought that eventually developed into today's dominant strain of economic thinking.

Tocqueville's broad perspective is apparent in the "Memoir on Pauperism." The "Memoir" echoes Rousseau in its description of how human beings in a state of savagery are equals, until private property, and especially land-ownership, are created. Inequality immediately results. But whereas Rousseau thinks everything is downhill from there, Tocqueville adopts the more optimistic perspective found in Montesquieu, Smith and Say. For Rousseau, inequality inevitably grows ever greater. Tocqueville modified Rousseau's account with a depiction of equality at the end of the story. Savages are equals, and "very civilized men can all become equal because they all have at their disposal similar means of attaining comfort and happiness. Between these two extremes is found inequality . . ." The modern world has clearly arrived at the end of the period of inequality. Democratic society, based on equality, is now at hand ("Memoir," 1997, 20).

Tocqueville also departs from Rousseau by hailing the new needs human beings felt for better food, clothing, shelter and luxuries of all sorts. Rousseau had condemned each perceived new need as yet another degradation of the body and soul. Not so Tocqueville. For him it is a good thing that "the poor and the rich, each in his sphere, conceive of new enjoyments which were unknown to their ancestors." It is good that "an immense number of new commodities have been introduced into the world . . . The life of the farmer became more pleasant and comfortable, the life of the great proprietor more varied and more ornate; comfort was available to the majority" (22).[1]

---

[1] Say also makes this point.

But "these happy results have not been obtained without a necessary cost." The new needs present a paradoxical danger. "The more prosperous a society is, the more diversified and more durable become the enjoyments of the greatest number, the more they simulate true necessity through habit and imitation. Civilized man is therefore infinitely more exposed to the vicissitudes of destiny than savage man." A savage complains when he is starving. A civilized man complains when he can't have dessert. The civilized man therefore has many more occasions for complaint. This is a Rousseauian argument, but Tocqueville, unlike Rousseau, emphasizes that the balance is on the whole positive. It is one of Tocqueville's merits that the positive does not blind him to the negative – and to the threats to freedom that may derive from it. In a democratic society, the "Memoir" tells us, poor people will feel especially deprived, and this dissatisfaction may lead them to revolution. This same point will come up in his *Recollections* of the revolutions of 1848 (22, 24).

Alongside increased feelings of deprivation, Tocqueville points out another economic problem that cannot be avoided in a democratic society. The development of civilization leads ever more people to leave the farm to work in the new factories that cater to these needs. This process is inevitable with the social and physical mobility that comes with democracy (23). But industry is a riskier business than agriculture. As needs grow, as industry grows, more and more people risk sudden unemployment due to the rise and fall of the business cycle. Their greater needs make the resulting deprivations strike them all the more keenly. Further, the number of people in absolute poverty, unable to feed themselves, also rises. The paradox is that:

As long as the present movement of civilization continues, the standard of living of the greatest number will rise; society will become more perfected, better informed; existence will be easier, milder, more embellished, and longer. But at the same time we must look forward to an increase of those who will need to resort to the support of their fellow men to obtain a

small part of these benefits. It will be possible to moderate this
double movement . . . but no one can stop it. (25)

What can be done to "moderate" this movement? Tocqueville
looks for remedies, and to some extent finds them in the same
places he had in America, in association, enlightened self-
interest and religion.

Tocqueville distinguished, not always clearly, between three
different ways of helping the poor: legal charity, private charity
and public charity. Legal charity (which he also sometimes called
public charity, confusingly) guarantees the poor a right to relief,
a right to work and/or subsistence provided by the government.
Private charity is provided by individuals and private associations. Public charity is provided by the government, but only in
exceptional circumstances or to deal with specific problems,
such as natural disasters, schooling or old age.

Tocqueville starts by considering legal charity: "At first glance,
there is no idea that seems more beautiful and grander . . ." But
people (not just the poor) have "a natural passion for idleness."
They only work for two reasons: "the need to live and the desire
to improve the conditions of life." Unfortunately, only a "small
minority" want to rise in the world. The result is poor people who
do not want to work, and who if they have to work to live have
little or no interest in saving the money that might allow them to
escape poverty. This makes legal charity a permanent subsidy to
"those who do nothing or who make bad use of their labor."
In practice society's noble impulse to take care of its least fortunate has evil results. "Is it possible to escape the fatal consequences of a good principle? For myself I consider them inevitable
. . . Any measure that establishes legal charity on a permanent
basis and gives it an administrative form thereby creates an idle
and lazy class . . ." Giving the poor a legal right to state assistance
was bad for the economy and bad for their souls (19, 26–28, 30).

But Tocqueville is not willing to let the question rest there.
"Who would dare to let a poor man die of hunger because it's
his own fault that he is dying? Who will hear his cries and reason

about his vices" (28). Tocqueville will not play the role of Mr. Scrooge. The first alternative he considers is private charity. Tocqueville discusses several forms of private charity in the "Memoir," more or less repeating themes found in *Democracy* under the heading of the uses of association, enlightened self-interest and religion. He suggests that charity plays an important role in binding rich and poor together in democratic society. But he concludes that private philanthropy, meritorious and useful as it is, cannot be relied upon. It is not enough, has never been enough and will become ever more inadequate: "Individual charity seems quite weak when faced with the progressive development of the industrial classes and all the evils that civilization joins to the inestimable goods it produces" (37).

France needs something in between "legal charity," which does too much harm, and private charity, which does not do enough good. Tocqueville thus accepts the idea of "public charity." He recognizes "not only the utility but the necessity of public charity applied to inevitable evils such as the helplessness of infancy, the decrepitude of old age, sickness, insanity. I even admit its temporary usefulness in times of public calamities . . . I even understand that public charity which opens free schools for the children of the poor . . ." (36). Although Tocqueville opens the next paragraph by arguing "that any permanent regular administrative system whose aim will be to provide for the needs of the poor will breed more miseries than it can cure," he had already justified a quite extensive list of government interventions, which together amount to something akin to the "social safety net" of the twentieth century or, more modestly, to the Bismarckian social insurance schemes of the late nineteenth. They certainly went far beyond reality. Too far, perhaps. Such ideas, when they were at all respectable in 1835, were far too associated with Catholic Legitimism to be politically comfortable for Tocqueville (37). This is perhaps the reason he abandoned them in his unfinished "Second Memoir on Pauperism."

Instead, in the "Second Memoir" Tocqueville stresses the moral importance of property-ownership, a more politically cautious strategy. He praises the French pattern of small-landholding over the large estates found in England, maintaining that the moral and political benefits of peasant landownership far outweigh any economic disadvantages it might have, and indeed contesting whether it did have economic drawbacks (Keslassy 186–87).

However, for Tocqueville industrialism was the wave of the future, and proletarians, not peasants, were his main concern. What could be done to "guaranty the industrial classes both against the ills they bring on themselves and those about which they can do nothing"? The implicit further question is what can be done to protect society against the industrial classes? In the "Second Memoir" the solution to both questions is to promote the acquisition of property by the proletariat. Tocqueville suggests several ways of doing this. Notably, he thinks that one day it will be practical for workers to create successful manufacturing cooperatives of their own, but that at present this is impossible. Instead, therefore, Tocqueville suggests that the government create a combination savings bank/pawn shop for the poor, which will pay above-market interest rates to attract deposits, and use the deposits to give loans at below-market rates, thus helping the poor at both ends. This would encourage the poor to accumulate the capital necessary to make them independent of the swings of the market for factory labor. A worthy plan, but one hardly likely to have a major impact. Perhaps Tocqueville thought so, too. He abandoned the "Second Memoir" without finishing it ("Second Memoir," 2005, 5–10).

Three years later, in the second volume of *Democracy in America*, published in 1840, Tocqueville returned to the subjects of poverty and industrial development in democratic societies. He retains much of the economic perspective of the memoirs on pauperism. He continues to regard industrialism as the wave of the future, and industrial crises as endemic and unavoidable. He addresses the threat they may pose to freedom. However, in *Democracy*, when Tocqueville considers social and economic issues, his perspective is primarily from the top down, rather than the bottom up. Although he describes a brutalized proletariat, he primarily examines the dangers to freedom that might be presented by a new industrial aristocracy, or by increased government ownership of industry. Although most commentators on Tocqueville have concentrated on the industrial aristocracy, it is the government that Tocqueville considers the greatest threat.

The threat a new industrial aristocracy posed to freedom is described in the chapter titled "How Industry Could Give Rise To An Aristocracy." It was this chapter that served Tocqueville's defenders in periods when Marxism was dominant and readers wanted to know what Tocqueville had to say about the bourgeoisie. Here at least Tocqueville seemed to have briefly trod the same path as the author of the *Communist Manifesto*.

Marx and Tocqueville come closest in the picture they paint of an oppressed and impoverished proletariat, perhaps due to a common source in Adam Smith's account of the division of labor in *The Wealth of Nations*. In Tocqueville's version, "as the principle of division of labor is more thoroughly applied, the worker becomes weaker, more limited, and more dependent. The art progresses, the artisan regresses." As he sums it up, "What should we expect of a man who has spent twenty years of his life making pinheads?" "The man is degraded as the workman is perfected." These degraded workers become more vulnerable as their specialized skills become irrelevant. "Before long, the worker has no need of anything but physical strength without intelligence." Tocqueville could have drawn extensive conclusions from this picture, a picture he admits is at odds with his account of a democratic society in which equality is ever-increasing. But he stops short, partly because, unlike for Marx, for Tocqueville the industrial proletariat is a minority and an exception within democratic society. Tocqueville's proletariat is an object of pity, rather than the motor of history. The further we go on in Tocqueville's chapter, the more the resemblance to Marx fades (*Democracy*, 2004, 649–50).

Tocqueville then switches his attention from the worker to his master. For Marx, the bourgeoisie are the lords of capitalism, predestined to rule until the communist revolution. For Tocqueville, this new industrial aristocracy "is an exception, a monster, in relation to the social state as a whole." The resemblance between capitalism and feudalism is only superficial. The worker may look like a serf, dressed in the same rags, but how different is the lord! "The poor have few ways of escaping their condition and becoming rich, but the rich are always becoming poor or quitting business with the profits they have amassed. Thus the elements of the poor class are fixed, but the elements of the rich class are not." There is no permanence in this new master class, unlike in feudalism. There is also no true social hierarchy: "Not only are the rich not solidly united among themselves, but there is no genuine bond between the poor man and the rich man." The idea of such an industrial "aristocracy" actually governing a country appears ridiculous to Tocqueville, not least because the industrialist, unlike the feudal lord, has no interest in government. Tocqueville describes the industrial aristocracy as "one of the harshest that has ever existed on earth. But it is also one of the most limited and least dangerous." The industrialists pose little threat to democracy or freedom (651–52).

What Tocqueville really fears from industry in democratic society is not its owners or its workers, but the government, which may or may not claim to act on their behalf. The state is the greatest threat to freedom. It is to the state, not to the factory-owners or the proletariat, that he returns at the end of the book, in the chapter on "How Sovereign Power in Today's European Nations is Increasing, Although Sovereigns Are Less Stable." Among the many causes of increased government power that Tocqueville discusses in this chapter he singles out "one major cause, which, independently of all that I have mentioned thus far, constantly contributes to expanding the action of the sovereign and increasing his prerogatives. Not enough attention has been paid to it. That cause is the development of industry . . ." (809).

Tocqueville contrasts industrial enterprises with landownership. Landownership, the former bulwark of the aristocracy, was protected against government encroachment in multiple ways. Land gave its owners, whether peasants or dukes, a measure of independence from the government. Not so industrial property. "The industrial class," that is, those, rich and poor, who owed their livelihoods to industry, "has not become less dependent as it has become more numerous. On the contrary, it seems to carry despotism within itself, and despotism naturally spreads as the industrial class develops" (809–10).

Tocqueville gives the mining industry as an example of the dependence of modern industrial property on the state. Mines had once been property like any other. But the state had gradually extended control over mines, often effectively confiscating them, so that "the owners were transformed into users. They received their rights from the state, and, what is more, the state claimed the power to direct them almost everywhere." As the mining industry continued to grow and develop in nineteenth-century Europe, this meant that "sovereigns are daily extending their domain beneath our feet and populating it with their servants" (809n.5). State control of the mining industry seemed inevitable.

Mines were just one example among many. Industrializing Europe needed more "roads, canals, ports, and other works of a semi-public nature." Because of the vast sums needed, private individuals were increasingly unable to create these things on their own, so that "the obvious tendency for all sovereigns nowadays is to assume the sole responsibility for undertakings of this kind, thereby constricting the independence of the populations they rule more and more each day." In economic life, association was a weak barrier against despotism. Industrial associations, for example, corporations, were more subject to regulation by the state than individuals, because the public did not consider such regulations to be an infringement of personal freedom, as they would have regarded similar regulations on, for example, religious or political associations. Individuals do not protest when corporations are regulated by the government, because they often "look upon such badly needed associations with secret feelings of fear and jealousy . . . they come close to seeing the free use that such associations make of their natural faculties as a dangerous kind of privilege." Surely this is one of Tocqueville's most accurate, yet least well-known predictions! The end result is that "sovereigns thus increasingly appropriate the greater part of the new force that industry is creating in the world today and put it to their own use. Industry leads us, and they lead it" (810–12).[2]

The great threat to freedom the industrial revolution created was thus not the proletariat, nor yet the bourgeoisie. It was state socialism, imposed from above, that Tocqueville feared, the state taking control of the economy, at least of its industrial part, and thus controlling the lives of a large and growing part of the population. Centralization returns to Tocqueville's focus at the end of volume two of *Democracy*, a new kind of economic centralization for which Tocqueville is afraid that association will be an insufficient remedy. The second volume of *Democracy*, rather than continuing Tocqueville's reflections on poverty, was the beginning of his reflection on the danger of socialism.

Tocqueville remained concerned with the threats to freedom that arose from both the top and the bottom of democratic industrial societies. In 1843 he argued in a newspaper piece that the growth of the industrial proletariat and its exceptional status in democratic society posed a threat to freedom, although only in a distant future: "From them future revolutions will doubtless arise throughout the civilized world as well as in France. But these dangers are still very far off." Poverty might result, in the distant future, in revolutions designed to redistribute property. Socialism, not mentioned by name in the "Memoirs," was now

---

[2] See also the chapter Tocqueville drafted and eventually rejected, "Of the Manner In Which American Governments Act Toward Associations," in which he wavers on the extent to which governments in democratic societies need to become involved in private associations in order to make sure that certain kinds of necessary economic projects are practical, and the consequences this might have. This chapter is included in the Schleifer translation of the Nolla edition of *Democracy*.

a danger from below as well as from above. Tocqueville also continued to worry about helping the poor, partly to avoid such revolutions.

Plans for dealing with the problem of industrial poverty were at the heart of Tocqueville's unsuccessful project of forming a new political party in 1847. Although the embryo party, the "Young Left," never fought an election or attracted more than a couple of dozen parliamentary supporters, these plans prompted Tocqueville to write the document known as "Fragments for a Social Policy." Simply by having such proposals the party would differentiate itself from the others, generally mute on these questions. Tocqueville hoped to strike the public imagination, and it is significant that he chose to strike it in this particular way. The "Fragments for a Social Policy" show the development of Tocqueville's views since the "Memoir on Pauperism" (Keslassy 205–11).

The "Fragments" begin with considerations about how to reform the French tax system. Tocqueville's goal is to burden the poor as lightly as possible. He lists four principles. 1) It should entirely exempt the poorest people. 2) It should not tax necessities, "because then everyone is obliged to pay and the poor are burdened." 3) If you have to tax necessities or near-necessities, make the tax as low as possible.[3] 4) If the tax is high, "try to make it proportional to the wealth of the taxpayer." Tocqueville also considers tariffs, and recognizes that free trade would be better for the poor – but he notes that it would be political suicide to attempt to lower France's duties on agricultural products (*Reader*, 2002, 224).

Progressive taxation is thus on Tocqueville's agenda, with the crucial proviso that it is not intended to give money to the poor (e.g., legal charity), but to take less from them. The next section of the "Fragments" concerns other direct and indirect means of

---

[3] Reflecting his interest in legal questions, he sees court fees in the same light, since they are the same for all, and "a trial is often as necessary a commodity for the poor man as for the rich."

helping the poor. This section is difficult to interpret, because while Tocqueville provides an extensive list of means by which the poor might be helped, he never actually says he supports any, and from earlier and later writings it is clear that he opposed some. Nevertheless, he concludes that merely decreasing the tax burden on the poor "is a lot, but not enough." He goes on to say that "the true meaning of the revolution is equality, the more equal distribution of the goods of this world . . . People claim that the new government and the middle class which remains the governing class will not fulfill its duty in this. Is this true?" But after some more rhetoric of this kind, the document ends with this: "Sinister picture that people draw of the future, imminent perils . . . I don't believe any of it. What is serious is distant, but no less serious" (226).

What are we to make of this? It is significant that Tocqueville wanted to include a social plank in his projected party platform. He volunteered to introduce tax reform legislation himself, and even did so, at least to the extent of proposing a declaration of intent to lower taxes on the poor. For his time, he was clearly progressive, particularly with regard to the tax system. But, as the events of 1848 and his response to them make clear, he continued to believe that the greater threat to freedom came not from poverty, but from government tyranny in the name of eliminating poverty.

Tocqueville's *Recollections* describe the events of this period, and reflect on social questions. The events of June 1848, an uprising of the Paris poor with socialist overtones, provoked a strong response from Tocqueville, both in the *Recollections* and in the National Assembly. France had been through a lot of revolutions and attempted revolutions. What distinguished the June events was that their "object was not to change the form of the government, but to alter the organization of society." This was the result of the spread of socialist ideas among the poor, in particular, the attitude that "the goods of the wealthy were in some way the result of a theft committed against [the poor]." Tocqueville himself considered it possible that radical modifications would one day be made to the rights of property. As he put it in the

Recollections, "I am tempted to the belief that what are called necessary institutions are only institutions to which one has grown accustomed, and that in matters of social constitutions the field of possibilities is much wider than people living within each society imagines." But this judgment was not intended as an endorsement of socialism. Rather, in the aftermath of the June Days Tocqueville gave voice to one of the greatest parliamentary attacks on socialism of all time (*Recollections*, 1987, 75–76, 136–37).

Tocqueville's attack on socialism came in what is known as his "speech on socialism" or "speech on the right to work," delivered on September 12, 1848. He was responding to a proposed constitutional amendment that would have guaranteed every Frenchman the right to work and a job. In Tocqueville's view this would have required the government to become the universal employer "and finally the sole proprietor of everything," or at least to "become the great and only organizer of labor." In other words, establishing a right to work meant establishing socialism.[4]

Socialism, for Tocqueville, came in many varieties, but they all possessed three traits in common: an appeal to purely material-istic passions, a direct or indirect attack on the principle of private property and, most importantly, "a profound mistrust of liberty, of human reason . . . what characterizes all socialism is an incessant effort to mutilate, to cut off, to distort human freedom of all kinds; it is the idea that the state should be not only the director of society, but . . . the master of each man." Far from being the road to freedom, socialism was "the road to serfdom," in the phrase that the conservative thinker Friedrich von Hayek famously borrowed from Tocqueville.[5]

Tocqueville chose the comparison between socialism and serfdom advisedly. In his view, socialism was a reversion to a previous stage of history. Partly to needle his adversaries, he compared socialism to old-regime France. Under the old regime, the state had acted as every person's guardian. The French

---

[4] A partial version of this speech is available online at several websites. A complete translation is to be found as an appendix to Watkins (2003, 571–82).
[5] "Serfdom" is Hayek's translation of "servitude."

Revolution had freed humanity from those fetters. The socialists wanted to put the shackles back on. Tocqueville also contrasted socialism and the Revolution by arguing that the revolutionaries, unlike the socialists, had appealed to nobler desires than mere material needs. As his clinching argument, he pointed to America as the country that was both the most democratic and the most hostile to socialism. This was proof that "Socialism and democracy are not interdependent concepts. They are not only different, but opposing philosophies . . . Democracy extends the sphere of personal independence, socialism confines it . . . Democracy and socialism have but one thing in common – equality. But note well the difference. Democracy aims at equality in liberty. Socialism desires equality in constraint and servitude." As he put it in some notes, "socialism is a new form of slavery" (*Reader*, 2002, 250).

However, Tocqueville's opposition to socialism did not make him into a doctrinaire opponent of government intervention in socioeconomic matters. It is often overlooked, or treated as mere window-dressing, that in the same speech he supported the idea of introducing "charity into politics." In fact, however, this had been the idea behind his 1847 draft political program. In the 1848 speech Tocqueville attributed to the French Revolution the idea of "duty to the poor, towards the suffering." While there was nothing in this "which forces the state to substitute itself in the place of individual foresight and caution, in place of the market . . . nothing in it which authorizes the state to meddle in the affairs of industry, or to impose its rules on it . . ." help for the suffering was not socialism, "but Christian charity applied in the political realm." In 1848 Tocqueville was once again attempting to apply American remedies to French democracy. His speech on socialism attempted to reconcile democracy and religion, the French Revolution with Christianity, in the claim that both commanded society to help the poor and to reject socialism. He continued to maintain this view after 1848. In 1853, he concluded of government help for the poor: "I am more and more of the opinion that we cannot avoid doing something of the kind. Humanity and public health make a law of it" (*OR*, 2001b, 368).

In economic questions, as everywhere else in his work, Tocqueville looked for remedies to the threats democratic society posed to freedom. Against such threats he naturally turned to the remedies he had discovered in America, the world's most democratic, freest and least socialist country: associations, enlightened self-interest and religion – and, above all, freedom. He encouraged charitable associations, motivated by enlightened self-interest and religious spirit. He supported tax reform and even limited government intervention, in the name of the Revolution and Christian charity. These remedies, however, did not seem to Tocqueville himself to be sufficient against the double threat freedom faced in democratic industrial societies, from mass poverty and state socialism. The passages in which he wonders about the future of private property might lead one to conclude that after 1848 he became as pessimistic about the future of the free market as about other kinds of freedom, at least in France. Aristocrat that he was, he took some comfort from the bourgeoisie's discomfort. Tocqueville's many expressions of distaste for the middle classes and the commercial spirit may well lead one to conclude that with a friend like this, capitalism had no need of enemies.

Yet Tocqueville is a friend of the free market as he is a friend of all freedoms. Socialism, no matter how "democratic," is not an acceptable option for him, because of the limitations it imposes on individual freedom. When dealing with poverty, freedom remains uppermost in Tocqueville's mind. However, poverty itself, in particular the growing urban poverty linked to industrialization, is also a threat to freedom. Because it is a threat to freedom, Tocqueville advocates forceful action to deal with it, including tax reform and even state economic intervention. In this Tocqueville goes well beyond what the typical French liberal politician of his day endorsed. With regard to social questions as to so much else, Tocqueville is a liberal of a new kind.

What kind of liberal was that?

7

Tocqueville, the Neo-Liberal

The word "liberal" is as confusing as it is unavoidable. This is the case today as well as in Tocqueville's time. Entire books have been devoted to explaining what it means to be a liberal, who is or was one, who isn't or wasn't. The same author or politician becomes or ceases to be a liberal depending on who is doing the viewing and when. Whether it is a good or bad thing to be a liberal depends very much on who is commenting, and on historical and geographical context. This is true of many such words, but of none more so than "liberal."

To add to the confusion in Tocqueville's case, he called himself a "liberal of a new kind." He meant some specific things by this, such as his view that religion and freedom were natural allies, a view that, to say the least, was uncommon among those called liberals in France in 1835. More generally, he meant that his liberalism was that of a man in and of a democratic society, a man devoted to freedom in a world based on democratic equality. In Tocqueville's lifetime, democracy was a new context for the only meaning "liberal" has always retained, commitment to freedom as a value of the highest order. This is the oldest sense of the word, part of its etymology from the Latin "liber," meaning "free."

However, Tocqueville's liberalism was new for more reasons than his differences from the people called liberals in France in his time. Tocqueville's liberalism was new because his understanding of the world, and of freedom, was new. He was a neo-liberal,[1] surrounded by liberals, conservatives, democrats and socialists, none of whom sympathized with all his concerns, few of whom, he felt, understood any of them. For all the ideas he borrowed from the intellectual commonplaces of the day, Tocqueville's neo-liberalism, far from embodying his time, responded to a world that had not yet quite arrived.

"Neo" means "new" or "revived." Tocqueville's neo-liberalism is both of these, new compared to what had gone before, and revived for a society that was becoming democratic. But "neo-liberalism" means more than this. Tocqueville stands at the very beginning of a new tradition within the history of liberal thought, one that is later incarnated (more or less) in the "New Liberalism" of fin-de-siècle England, "Solidarism" in France, in pre–World War I Germany the movement that surrounded Friedrich Naumann and after World War I the "Ordo-Liberals," and in 1930s America the ideas of people like Walter Lippmann. While these individuals and movements did not necessarily acknowledge Tocqueville as an ancestor (as the next chapter shows, Tocqueville exercised limited influence in the decades immediately after his death), they nonetheless worked in the neo-liberal tradition that begins with him.

Tocqueville's neo-liberalism possesses three dimensions that had not previously been combined in liberal thought, or at least, since it is always hazardous to make claims about who came first, not in so authoritative a form. These relate to economics, society and morality. It is the addition of these dimensions to its conception of freedom that puts the "neo" in neo-liberalism, and makes Tocqueville a neo-liberal. In 1830, or 1840, or 1850, most liberals and anti-liberals would not have considered these dimensions of freedom central to liberalism. Liberalism then was much more

---

[1] The word "neo-liberal" itself has a complicated history, dating back to at least the 1930s. At present, it is most frequently used outside the United States, to describe partisans of free-market economics, and almost never used at all in American domestic politics. The meaning given the term here is described later.

absorbed in lists of constitutional rights, suffrage questions, questions of representative government and the separation of powers. Liberalism today is still mostly devoted to "rights-talk." Tocqueville, of course, cares deeply about these things as well. The economic, social and moral dimensions neo-liberalism adds to traditional liberal concerns are additions, not substitutions. Their content, as found in Tocqueville's writings, can be summarized as follows:

1) The economic dimension of freedom. Before 1850, the word "liberal" had little association with views about economics. Today it has strong, but different, economic implications on the two sides of the Atlantic. In the United States, following from the tradition that a liberal, a supporter of freedom, is one who opposes orthodoxy, it means someone who favors government intervention in the economy. Since orthodox economists oppose this, liberals are those who favor it. In Europe, on the other hand, a liberal, one who supports freedom, favors the free market, and thus in Europe liberalism is identified with an economy free from political interference. Tocqueville stands astride this divide. He favors the free market as an integral part of human freedom, but leaves space for government intervention in specific areas, and for a tax system not merely proportional but favorable to the poor. In contemporary terms, he was committed to a market economy, with a social safety net constructed out of both private and public elements. The late-twentieth-century French Socialist politician Lionel Jospin actually described economic neo-liberalism in this Tocquevillean sense very well in his phrase "yes to a market economy, no to a market society." This is a neo-liberal attitude, although of course Jospin, a French Socialist, never thought of it that way – or if he did, knew better politically than to say so in a country where the word "liberal," in all its forms, is usually reserved for despised Anglo-Saxon reactionaries.

2) The social dimension of freedom. The neo-liberal vision of freedom, Tocqueville's vision of freedom, insists that freedom has both public and private components, which include both

freedom from interference, and participation in communities. Tocqueville implicitly endorsed Constant's idea of modern freedom, in which the individual asks first of all to be left alone, allowed to act independently on his or her own initiative, without interference from the community or the government. The tyranny of the majority and government despotism are anathema to him. Like Constant, Tocqueville conceived of modern politics as a means of providing guaranties for individual freedom. However, Tocqueville's notion of a free life is not based to the same degree as Constant's on individual independence. Tocqueville's notion of freedom has a social dimension. For Tocqueville, a free life is not lived outside political and private associations. His human being, like Aristotle's, is a political animal. Freely chosen individual participation in society is essential if the society is to be free, and essential if the individual is to be free. But unlike Aristotle's beast, Tocqueville's democratic animal has other drives of equal or greater importance than politics. Modern democratic life means that participation in communities will, for most people, be on a limited scale and involve limited, though real, commitment. This vision of freedom has links with both traditionally conservative views, and to communitarian perspectives on the left. It is largely this aspect of Tocqueville's neo-liberalism that has made him attractive to both the left and the right.

3) The moral dimension of freedom. Tocqueville treats freedom as a moral value, a holy thing that involves a commitment that goes beyond enlightened self-interest. As he put it, "I would have loved liberty in all times, I think, but at the present time I am inclined to worship it" (*Democracy*, 2004, 822). His is a religion of freedom. Neo-liberalism can be combined with other faiths, indeed in Tocqueville's view probably must be combined with other faiths to be successful, but it involves a deep moral commitment to freedom. No one ever dies on a barricade for free trade, few take up arms to defend their constitutional rights, but many people have and will fight and die for freedom, as they have fought and died in the name of other deities. However, the moral commitment to freedom Tocqueville espoused was more

than just a willingness to fight for it on a barricade, a situation that after all does not come up very often. It is an attitude that sees the daily exercise of freedom, the ordinary consciousness of being free to act, think and speak in both the public and the private sphere, as essential to a good life. It is this moral commitment to freedom that dissuades neo-liberals from, for example, devoting themselves to purely private concerns (e.g., individualism, in Tocqueville's sense of the word), and encourages them to pursue what Tocqueville considered "higher" values, of which the highest, by far, was freedom.

Tocqueville's neo-liberalism added these new economic, social and moral dimensions to the traditional mix of liberal goals and attitudes. His neo-liberalism was different from the older liberalisms that surrounded it, and this difference is partly responsible for Tocqueville's limited success. Of course, he was successful to some extent. He was a famous writer and a well-known politician, even a government minister, if never a prime minister. But his success fell below his ambitions and expectations. He wrote and acted in ways intended to address what he saw as his time and country's most pressing needs. But his understanding of those needs overlapped and went beyond his contemporaries' perceptions. Despite his efforts, his thought was not really very well adapted to his time. Tocqueville was the opposite of the man the German philosopher Hegel saw as the incarnation of the spirit of the age – Napoleon. It is fitting that unlike Napoleon, unlike even Napoleon III, Tocqueville could never dominate the hearts and minds, much less the politics, of his day. His neo-liberalism was not a good fit for his time. It may prove to be a better fit with ours.

Part III

8

Tocqueville and His Readers

"I please many people of conflicting opinions, not because they understand me, but because they find in my work, by considering it from a single side, arguments favorable to their passions of the moment" (*SL*, 1985, 99–100). Rarely has an author so accurately described the reception of his work, not only in his own day, but in ours. At first, however, Tocqueville was more afraid of pleasing no one than pleasing everyone. He did everything he could to make sure *Democracy in America* would be a success. He chose a publisher known for publishing popular novelists, such as Sir Walter Scott and Victor Hugo, and who had good press connections. But he did not leave his publicity campaign in his publisher's hands. He used his own connections, above all with Chateaubriand, to make sure *Democracy* was widely noticed. It was reviewed at length by all the important political periodicals and newspapers, if not always favorably. *Democracy in America* was a major success.

In France, six thousand copies of volume one of *Democracy* were printed in the five years after its publication in 1835. "Serious" works about politics more ordinarily sold only five hundred–one thousand copies. By comparison, novels sold in far greater numbers. Thus *Democracy* was a publishing success in context, but not a "best-seller."[1]

---

[1] Here and throughout this section I am much indebted to Mélonio (1998). The French version is much to be preferred.

In terms of the esteem and recognition it brought its author, however, Tocqueville had nothing to envy even a best-selling novelist such as Balzac. Indeed the opposite was the case. By 1842, Balzac was writing a thinly veiled caricature of Tocqueville as an author who had managed:

> To make a book that is moral, governmental, philosophic, philanthropic all at the same time, from which one can excerpt a few more or less fine-sounding pages for any occasion . . . His name can never again be spoken except accompanied by this long epithet: "Mister Marphurius[2] who did Germany and the Germans." It becomes a title, a fiefdom! And what a fief! It produces a swarm of decorations sent from every Court and entitles one to some section or another at the Institut. (Mélonio 31)

Tocqueville became, and has remained, "Mr. America." Almost immediately the imitations began – and have never stopped. In the years after 1835 many works on "Democracy and/in . . ." were published in France and elsewhere, while others attempted to capitalize on *Democracy*'s success by writing about America. In the French political world, Tocqueville's name became one to conjure with. The Académie Française awarded him a prestigious prize, and soon elected him to membership. Everyone wanted to cite a few of his melodious sentences on behalf of their pet political project – a habit that endures even today, especially in America.

Tocqueville also rapidly acquired another epithet to go along with "Mr. America": "the new Montesquieu." Half a dozen French critics made use of the comparison to Montesquieu in their reviews. It was not the result of erudite comparison, but more because they seemed to have an obvious affinity, both in subject and in style. Tocqueville's moralism also seemed to many

---

[2] Marphurius, described as a skeptical philosopher, is the name of a character in a play by the seventeenth-century French playwright Molière.

readers, even in 1835, slightly archaic in tone, which made comparison with a hallowed name of the past seem appropriate.

To become "Mr. America" in France is noteworthy, to achieve the same status in the United States even more so. Volume one of *Democracy* was not published in the United States until 1838 (in a pirated version of the British translation), but reviews of it, based on both the French original and the British translation, had appeared as early as 1836. The Americans, although not uncritical, were on the whole as impressed by Tocqueville as the French. This was partly because they were not used to praise from foreigners. Accounts of the United States published by European travelers, mostly British, in the early nineteenth century were usually highly critical, and often contemptuous. To be taken as a model society by a French aristocrat was deeply flattering.

There were certain aspects of *Democracy* that American critics rejected, however. In particular, as Tocqueville had predicted they would, they rejected the idea of the "tyranny of the majority" in America. They also, as well they might, found absurd Tocqueville's prediction that one day the American masses would become Catholic. Neither then nor since have Americans been quick to recognize that the book's target audience was French, and that much of what Tocqueville had to say was not really meant for their ears. On the other hand, American reviewers understood rather better than the French certain aspects of what Tocqueville had to say, in particular about the way in which religion worked hand-in-hand with democracy (and freedom) in the United States.[3]

Tocqueville's appeal to all ends of the political spectrum was not limited to France and America. In England the book was praised by radicals and by conservatives such as the Conservative party leader Sir Robert Peel. It was translated into several languages besides English, and the young Cavour, future prime minister of Italy, was much impressed. Of all the reviews Tocqueville received, one deserves special mention. It is very

---

[3] On Tocqueville's American reception, see Zunz (2006).

rare that a great book receives a review that is itself an important intellectual contribution. The reviews of both the first and second volumes of *Democracy* by John Stuart Mill are an example of this rare species. Mill's view of modern society was heavily influenced by Tocqueville, and his classic *On Liberty* (1859) is largely a meditation on themes from *Democracy*.

The publication of the second volume of *Democracy* in 1840 had results that, for Tocqueville, were disappointing. In 1835, his great success was unexpected. In 1840, the more equivocal reception of volume two was an unpleasant surprise. This was because, if volume one was regarded as "serious," its tales of American life nevertheless made it lighter reading than volume two. Reading the more abstract volume two seemed like hard work, as one reviewer put it. There were weightier obstacles to a favorable reception, however. Volume two was disliked by much of the French left. The less optimistic Tocqueville of the second volume was too conservative for their tastes, and those aspects of volume two that would appeal to later generations on the left, such as Tocqueville's criticism of mass culture, were not yet on the left's agenda. One issue in particular attracted the ire of many French reviewers of all political shades: religion. For some, Tocqueville was a friend of religion, but insufficiently partisan about which one, that is, not Catholic enough. For others, on both left and right, the very idea that Catholicism could be reconciled with democracy, in any sense of the word, was anathema. Volume two cemented Tocqueville's reputation as Mr. America, if only by adding a weighty piece of evidence to the pile, but it cannot be said to have broadened it. It did not, for example, provoke publication of an inexpensive French edition, which would have to await the revolution of 1848, when once again the American republic attracted public notice. Tocqueville's intellectual stock had reached a plateau in France at mid-century.

The American reviews of *Democracy* often lumped the two volumes together because of the short delay between their publication in America. They tended to ignore volume two altogether, perhaps put off by its abstraction. But if Tocqueville's intellectual reputation plateaued in France after 1840, this was not the case in America. In the early reviews of *Democracy*, Tocqueville's discussion of slavery and American race relations was not much appreciated. In the early 1850s, as the issue moved to the forefront of American politics, and still more with the outbreak of the American Civil War in 1861, Tocqueville's fears on the subject seemed ever more prescient. A new edition of *Democracy* was published in 1862, with a revised translation. In the same year the *New York Times* could refer to it as "known to every school boy . . . a classic on this side of the Atlantic." For Henry Adams, oddly enough, it took a trip to England in 1863 to expose him to Tocqueville's influence: "I have learned to think de Tocqueville my model and I study his life and works as the gospel of my private religion," he wrote. In this period Tocqueville took on, not for the last time, the function of a political oracle for many Americans. Charles Eliot Norton, writer and Harvard professor, was another of Tocqueville's disciples, and wrote an influential and laudatory review of the new edition for the *Atlantic Monthly*. Excerpts from Tocqueville were published in abolitionist journals such as *The Liberty Bell* and *The African Repository*. During the Civil War *Democracy*'s reputation in America reached the pinnacle where it has remained ever since.

In France, it was not the American Civil War that boosted Tocqueville's reputation, but publication of *The Old Regime* in 1856. Americans translated, published and praised the work, but interest was mostly limited to historians. In France, however, Tocqueville found again all the success of the first volume of *Democracy*, and more.

Circumstances played a role, even though, at first glance, they were not favorable. In 1835, when *Democracy* was published, Tocqueville was a rising young man known only for his work on prison reform. France, five years after the July Revolution, was full of interest in new political ideas. In 1856, Tocqueville was a not-very-successful ex-politician who had withdrawn from politics in opposition to Napoleon III's 1852 coup d'état. France was frightened of new ideas after the events of 1848, and evidently not much interested in political freedom. But beneath the surface, there was much in Tocqueville's favor. The liberal opposition needed a standard-bearer and a manifesto, but under the political censorship of the time, this could not be some new political program. However, a work on the French Revolution was another matter. In it Tocqueville could condemn the contemporary regime under the pretense of writing history, and he rarely let pass an opportunity to do so. *The Old Regime* gave Tocqueville a leading rank among French liberals he had never enjoyed before.

A total of 8,800 copies of *The Old Regime*, in four editions, were printed between June 1856 and December 1858. Demand for the book remained high through 1900, by which time 23,600 copies had been sold. Again Tocqueville had great success – in the high-brow market. Cheap editions of *The Old Regime* were not published in this period. The liberal opposition to Napoleon III dominated the high-brow press, and had nothing but praise for the book. Approval for the book further on the left was mixed with some distaste for Tocqueville's rejection of the Jacobins and pessimism about the future of freedom in France. As one favorable reviewer concluded, "It will be admired by everyone and will not satisfy anyone." The admiration, however, was almost universal among those who did not like the Second Empire. Friends of the Imperial regime, to which the author (and his book) was a sworn enemy, naturally loathed it. One Bonapartist compared him with Montesquieu, but as a "feeble descendant through the female line." A few Catholics were also unhappy with Tocqueville's criticism of the Church's connivance with the absolutist monarchy (Jardin, 505; Mélonio, 98-101).

Nevertheless, the book restored the glow to Tocqueville's intellectual reputation in France, and polished it more brightly than it had ever shone before. If the Americans did not pay too much attention to *The Old Regime*, in Europe it was in some respects more successful than *Democracy in America*. Translated into English while still in proof, it received a very warm reception in the English press. An estimated 1,000 copies of the first

English edition were sold, and the book was frequently cited over the generation to come. It was also widely reviewed in Germany. Perhaps most surprisingly, it made Tocqueville's reputation in Russia. Russians in the mid-nineteenth century (like Germans, but even more so) found many analogies between their situation and the old regime Tocqueville depicted. Tolstoy read Tocqueville, as did Russian government ministers. One Russian review went so far as to suggest putting the government Tocqueville described in his appendix on Languedoc into practice in Russia (Mélonio 109–10). By the time he died in 1859, Tocqueville's name was well-known throughout the Western world.

After his death, Tocqueville's reputation and influence fluctuated greatly. It was at its height in the decade or two immediately following his death, when he achieved the position he had never been able to conquer during his life – the acknowledged leader of the whole French liberal movement. But Tocqueville's fame suffered a steady eclipse from about 1880 until around 1960. While he was never entirely expelled from the French literary pantheon, he was certainly banished to a side-corridor.

In France, Tocqueville's posthumous reputation was partly the victim of his success. With the end of the Second Empire in 1870, and the consolidation of the Third Republic in 1875–79, he ceased to have obvious political relevance. Many of his ideas, their sharp edges ignored, faded into the commonplaces they derived from. Further, as America's image became increasingly tarnished in the French public's view, interest in *Democracy* faded. It was through the *Old Regime* that Tocqueville tended to maintain his diminishing foothold in French intellectual life. Some important French writers on the Revolution, such as Hyppolite Taine, continued to be influenced by him. Overall, however, as a history of his reception in France puts it, "Between 1870 and 1879 Tocqueville's works were still important; from 1880 to 1893 they were passé..." (Mélonio 151). Afterwards, for many decades he seemed of only historical interest, revived slightly by the posthumous (1893) publication of his *Recollections*.

Individual exceptions aside, if Tocqueville was still valued in France in 1893–1945, it was as a minor historian and moralist who had made some witty remarks about America and about virtue. It was not until the 1950s that Tocqueville's French reputation began to revive. Beginning in the 1950s, Tocqueville slowly began to seem relevant to contemporary life, as he had ceased to be after the 1870s. The first sign of a Tocqueville revival came in the form of a new edition of *The Old Regime* in 1952, with an introduction by a leading Marxist historian of the French Revolution, Georges Lefebvre. Raymond Aron, on the right-center of the French political spectrum, then took on the role of Tocqueville's champion. In some ways this was surprising. Aron, one of the few people who were ever seriously interested in *both* Marx and Tocqueville, confessed to being more attracted to Marx. Nevertheless he also recognized that the Europe of the 1960s, unlike the Europe of the 1930s, looked a lot more like the world Tocqueville had predicted than the one Marx had (the rise of Tocqueville's reputation, outside the United States, has been largely dependent on the decline of Marxism). In Aron's influential 1955 study, *Main Currents in Sociological Thought*, he boldly listed Tocqueville, along with Comte, Marx, Weber and Durkheim, among the founders of sociology. Aron created a national commission to publish Tocqueville's complete works (thirty plus volumes later, the commission is still at work in 2013).

Aron was exceptional among French students of Tocqueville because of the importance he gave *Democracy* in his evaluation of Tocqueville. In France, the next stage in the Tocqueville revival returned to the more usual source, *The Old Regime*. In 1967 the historian François Furet published *Interpreting the French Revolution*, which led to both a new understanding of the French Revolution and a return to Tocqueville, whose *Old Regime* was acknowledged by Furet as the main inspiration for his own work. Since that time, Tocqueville's influence in France has continued to increase, spreading beyond the history of the French Revolution to become, if not quite a replacement for Marx, at least a considerable presence throughout the French intellectual scene. The end of the Cold War and the collapse of French Marxism left only a pallid postmodernism as his rival.

In contrast with France, in America Tocqueville always seemed relevant.[4] Americans continued to recognize enough of themselves in *Democracy* to want to either dispute the portrait or use it. Although Tocqueville on slavery was of less interest after the Civil War and Reconstruction, this did not prevent publication of two new, handsome editions of *Democracy*, in 1898 and 1899, with introductions by two distinguished American intellectuals – John T. Bigelow, a former American ambassador to France, and Daniel Coit Gilman, founding president of Johns Hopkins University. Yet a third edition was published in 1900, with two introductions by senators, one a former Confederate general, the other a former Union colonel. Admiration for Tocqueville, it seems, has always had the ability to unite Americans of the most divergent political affiliations. In 1912 Tocqueville received the highest accolade American publishing had to bestow – publication of *Democracy* in a cheap textbook edition. A Tocqueville for the masses had finally arrived in America.[5]

If there was a dearth of new editions of Tocqueville in America between the World Wars, the large inventory built up in the years before World War I may have been responsible. At any event, he did not fade from view, and in 1945 a new translation of *Democracy* was published, and in 1955 a new translation of *The Old Regime*. By then, everyone was pointing to the passage in *Democracy* where Tocqueville referred to the United States and Russia as the great democratic powers of the future – one free, one not. Tocqueville was hailed as the prophet of the Cold War.

---

[4] Although an academic legend has grown up that his influence went into eclipse in America after the Civil War until World War II, this was not the case (Mancini 245–68).

[5] All these editions were reprinted, for a total of eleven different printings of *Democracy* between 1898 and 1912 (and a total of twenty-three between 1862 and 1912). Tocqueville was never absent from the shelves of American bookstores (Mancini).

When American intellectuals started to have misgivings about mass culture (e.g., David Riesman's classic *The Lonely Crowd* of 1953), volume two of Democracy was used as a model and source of convenient quotations. Marx's much smaller influence in America than France (and Europe) also helped Tocqueville maintain his American reputation. The American center-left of the 1960s and 1970s was particularly fond of Tocqueville, although that did not stop Republican presidents Nixon and Ford from quoting him. Tocqueville has continued to appeal to Americans on all sides of the political spectrum, but since the 1990s a rightwards shift in his appeal has been noticeable.[6] This shift has been accompanied, within the American intellectual world, by the growing influence of *The Old Regime* at the end of the twentieth century.

The converging lines of Tocqueville's reputation in France and America, and indeed the Western world, met in the celebrations that accompanied the 200th anniversary of his birth in 2005. A series of commemorative conferences was held from the United States to Japan, publications both academic and nonacademic multiplied and Tocqueville's status was officially confirmed in every way possible.

---

[6] A notable exception to the rightward shift is Sheldon S. Wolin.

Part IV

9

Tocqueville Today

At the beginning of the twenty-first century, Tocqueville's reputation and influence are probably greater than ever. In America, Tocqueville has become a fixture on both the political and the intellectual scene. He is quoted more often than any of the Founding Fathers, with the possible exception of Thomas Jefferson, who as author of the Declaration of Independence has an unfair advantage. He is cited at least as often as Abraham Lincoln, and almost as often as Martin Luther King. Every American president since Eisenhower has quoted him, and in 1995–96 alone, he was referred to on at least forty-five separate occasions in the United States Congress, twenty-six times by Republicans and nineteen times by Democrats. The American television network C-SPAN devoted a long series of programs to *Democracy in America* in 1997–98, including a bus tour across America retracing much of Tocqueville's route. For the website that accompanied the TV series, C-SPAN had no trouble coming up with the titles of fifty recent books that quoted him. The books' authors, not all Americans, included former British prime minister Margaret Thatcher and Republican congressional leader Newt Gingrich on the right, and former German chancellor Helmut Schmidt on the left. Typical of the American attitude to Tocqueville today is the title of a book published in 2001, *Tocqueville on American Character: Why Tocqueville's Brilliant Exploration of the American Spirit is as Vital and Important Today as It Was Nearly Two Hundred Years Ago* (Ledeen, 2001). Tocqueville has appeared regularly in the pages of *Time* magazine, and those

who give ten thousand dollars or more a year to the charitable
organization United Way are made members of its "Alexis de
Tocqueville Society." Investment funds are named after him. He
is by far the foreigner most honored in America today, well
ahead of his countryman Lafayette.

   Tocqueville's presence in American life is more than just
honorific, however, and his works are more than just a source
of convenient quotations by those who have never read him (the
American humorist Russell Baker once wrote that Americans
quote Tocqueville without ever having read him even more than
the Bible or Shakespeare). Recently a school of sociological
thought known as the "neo-Tocquevillians" has appeared,
inspired by Robert Putnam's 2000 publication of *Bowling Alone:
The Collapse and Revival of American Community*, derived from a
1995 article. In some respects the neo-Tocquevillians are simply
reviving the ideas of another prominent American sociologist
of the 1950s who was heavily influenced by Tocqueville, David
Riesman, author of *The Lonely Crowd*. Putnam revives Riesman's
vision of the solitary American, while adopting Tocqueville's
view of the importance of private associations, and lamenting
their decline in America, and the corresponding increase in
individualism. The neo-Tocquevillians have inspired considerable debate across the American political spectrum, with a corresponding interest in Tocqueville's works. Americans translated
Democracy in America three times in the decade 1998–2008, and
The Old Regime once (the English added another translation of
each in the same period).[1]

   All in all, the conclusion drawn by many American readers of
Tocqueville, and in particular of *Democracy in America*, is that
"reading Tocqueville today, it is as if he knew us in advance"
(*NYTimes*, May 30, 1998). Whether this is accurate or not is
almost irrelevant. What is significant is that so many Americans,

---

[1] See the American translations of *Democracy* by Mansfield and Winthrop,
Goldhammer and Schleifer, and of *The Old Regime* by Kahan and the English
translations by Bevan (see bibliography).

judging from Tocqueville's ubiquitous presence, think it is true. Nor is the judgment that Tocqueville understood America better than anyone limited to Americans. A review in the British newspaper *The Guardian* in 2004 suggested that "You simply cannot find a better book about the American character . . . It is so enlightened, so uncannily accurate, that it is impossible to gainsay even now" (Lezard 2004).

The influence of *Democracy* in the United States is not new, of course. More unusual on the America scene, from a historical perspective, is the contemporary influence of *The Old Regime.* Beginning in the 1970s, American historians of the French Revolution began engaging with Tocqueville, both for and latterly against, in a way they had never done before. Starting with the work of Keith Baker in the 1970s, Tocqueville's views of French history received a hearing in American academia they had never previously attained. If American politicians still don't quote *The Old Regime* very much, its influence has gradually spread among American political theorists and political philosophers.

In France, Tocqueville's reputation has continued to flourish since its revival by Aron and Furet. At the beginning of the twenty-first century appreciation for Tocqueville seems to be one of the few areas in which French and American culture are converging. Tocqueville has become almost as omnipresent on the French scene as on the American. In large part this is due to the eclipse of French Marxism. Certainly without it, it would have been difficult for Tocqueville's very different analysis of modernity to take center stage. One difference in recent French versus American appropriations of Tocqueville is interesting, however. Whereas in the United States, with the exception of Sheldon Wolin, Tocqueville's academic appropriation has come chiefly from the right, in France the left has also made a significant contribution to Tocqueville's reemergence, through the work of such figures as Claude Lefort.

Tocqueville's ideas are by no means uncontested in France, nor has the recent French attitude towards him always been uncritical. A number of recent studies have looked at his attitude to Algeria or to problems of poverty and social inequality and found them wanting. Nevertheless, "today in France, Tocqueville is the object of a kind of consensus . . . Tocqueville's chateau is a pilgrimage site for successive French presidents and ministers. The highest authorities in the land participate in Tocqueville prize ceremonies, and few writers have had the privilege of being the object of citations during ministry meetings, as Tocqueville has." In 2005 a book titled "*Tocqueville Aujourd'hui*," "*Tocqueville Today*" was published, which used Tocqueville's ideas to explain the latest French political controversies and their results. Tocqueville, it seems, was not only "uncannily accurate" about the America of two hundred years further on, he was just as accurate about France. In 2006 a prominent French philosopher felt the need to join the many other authors who have repeated Tocqueville's journey across America and sold books about it. This is cultural convergence indeed (Boudon; Lévy; Mélonio 189).

At the beginning of the twenty-first century Tocqueville's ideas have become central to the way both America and France understand themselves, as well as to many contemporary understandings of the democratic society we live in. What would have been most important to him, however, would have been the fact that the United States and above all France have finally achieved a durable combination of freedom and democracy. His question, perhaps, would have been whether they could indefinitely maintain this combination unless the rest of the world followed suit. And it is with respect to this question that perhaps the most interesting contemporary uses of Tocqueville's thought may be found.

Beyond his quotability, beyond the decline of Marxism, there is a reason why Tocqueville is so popular today. Tocqueville's lifelong project, the attempt to understand democracy, is what makes him so valuable to contemporary thinkers and politicians alike. His neo-liberalism seems right for the times. To recapitulate all the ways in which Tocqueville's investigations appeal to today's readers would be impossible, but those areas he focused on as remedies to the threats faced by freedom in democratic societies have proved to be of lasting interest in the post-Communist world.

Tocqueville's three remedies for the threats democracy poses to freedom, that is, association, religion and enlightened self-interest, all attract attention today. But of them all one has proved an especially fruitful field of discussion in the twenty-first century. This is his discussion of the role of associations in democratic societies. Through the idea of association, Tocqueville is central to modern discussions of "civil society," that is, those aspects of society independent of the state and of religion. The concept of civil society was not invented by Tocqueville, and owes much to other thinkers, particularly the nineteenth-century German philosopher G.W.F. Hegel. Nevertheless, today it is Tocqueville, rather than Hegel, who is usually appealed to when contemporary relevance is what matters. An internet search for the words "Tocqueville civil society" comes up with 154,000 references, even though Tocqueville only rarely used the words "civil society" (unlike Hegel, who gets 252,000 references when "Hegel civil society" is searched).

One of the main sources of interest in Tocqueville's discussion of association comes from people who want to promote political freedom and hope to find a recipe in Tocqueville's work, especially *Democracy in America*. This is particularly the case in parts of the world that have never experienced freedom, or long been deprived of it. Hence, since the end of the Cold War, interest in applied Tocqueville studies has emerged in places as diverse as Eastern Europe and South Korea (it is no accident that the University of Lodz, Poland, possesses an "Alexis de Tocqueville Center of Political and Legal Thought"). This results in articles with titles such as "Tocqueville's Missionaries: Civil Society Advocacy and the Promotion of Democracy" (Encarnacion), and projects such as the one the American Enterprise Institute, a conservative American think-tank, has directed about Tocqueville and China. While this has promoted interest in Tocqueville, it has not necessarily promoted a close reading of his works. His emphasis on the role association plays in political education is often, necessarily, subordinated in those trying to convince despotic regimes that independent charitable organizations are harmless. Regardless, contemporary interest in civil society has promoted both lip-service and serious inquiry into Tocqueville's ideas.

Among his other remedies to the ills of democracy, Tocqueville's attempt to link religion and freedom is still controversial. While some, particularly Americans, continue to find it plausible, the rise of Islamic fundamentalism has done little to convince skeptics that Tocqueville was right. Indeed, his relatively hostile (though by no means rigid) attitude to Islam has been of some comfort to those who would like to limit the positive link between religion and freedom to Christianity or the Judaeo-Christian tradition. Certainly, when Westerners try to apply Tocquevillian encouragement to the development of freedom in the Middle East or South Asia, religion itself has rarely been the tool of choice, although faith-based organizations are another matter. Here, as in his own time, it is largely Americans who have picked up on Tocqueville's attempt to unite freedom with the altar.

As far as the final remedy, enlightened self-interest, goes, the use made of it today is varied. Those interpreters who attempt to apply Tocqueville to the contemporary world may be broadly divided between those who emphasize those aspects of Tocqueville's thought favorable to the free market, and those who emphasize its more communitarian and anti-materialistic aspects. The emphasis placed on the role of self-interest in Tocqueville's thought varies accordingly. The role of enlightened self-interest in promoting freedom, however, tends to be merged with the role of associations. The argument is that enlightened self-interest will encourage people to join associations, and so on. Where Tocqueville has often been ignored, however, in this regard, is in the stress he places on directly political association. In his view it is the habit of political association that encourages economic association, far more than the other way around. Again, it has often been in the interest of those who wish to encourage civil society in China, for example, to downplay this aspect of Tocqueville's thought, even if in the final analysis they see the cultivation of association and of enlightened views of self-interest as a means of eventually democratizing the country's government. Even if he could not always agree with their interpretations of his thought, Tocqueville would certainly not have objected to contemporary efforts to adapt his work to the task of encouraging freedom today. Indeed, he would have felt deeply flattered. But as flattered as he might have been, it is hard to imagine him being any less concerned today than when he died in 1859 for the future of freedom in a democratic world. For insofar as Tocqueville has remained relevant, it is because we too live in a democratic world where the future of freedom is not assured.

Part V

Works Cited

This list is provided for readers' convenience in finding the references in the text. Readers should note that in the text *Oeuvres complètes* is abbreviated as *OC*, and *Selected Letters* as *SL*.

Aron, Raymond, 1968, *Main Currents in Sociological Thought*, Penguin, New York.

Baker, R., 1976, "Off the Top of de Tocq," The *New York Times*, 23 November.

Boudon, R., 2005, *Tocqueville Aujourd'hui*, Odile Jacob, Paris.

Craiutu, A., 1999, "Tocqueville and the Political Thought of the Doctrinaires," History of Political Thought, vol. 20, no. 3, 456–93.

Drescher, S., 1964, *Tocqueville and England*, Harvard, Cambridge.

Drolet, M., 2003, *Tocqueville, Democracy, and Social Reform*, Palgrave, Houndmills, Basingstoke.

Encarnacion, O.G., 2000, "Tocqueville's Missionaries: Civil Society Advocacy and the Promotion of Democracy," in *World Policy Journal*, March.

Furet, François, 1981, *Interpreting the French Revolution*, trans. Elborg Forster, Cambridge University, Cambridge.

Gannett, Jr., R., 2003, *Tocqueville Unveiled: The Historian and His Sources for The Old Regime and the Revolution*, University of Chicago, Chicago.

Gobineau, Arthur de, 1967, *The Inequality of Human Races*, H. Fertig, New York.

Guellec, L., 2004, *Tocqueville et les langages de la démocratie*, Honoré Champion, Paris.

Jardin, A., 1988, *Tocqueville: A Biography*, trans. L. Davis with R. Hemenway, Peter Halban, London.

Jaume, L., 2008, *Tocqueville: Les sources aristocratiques de la liberté*, Fayard, Paris.

Kahan, A.S., 1985, "Tocqueville's Two Revolutions," *Journal of the History of Ideas*, vol. 46, no. 4, 585–96.

—2001, *Aristocratic Liberalism: The Social and Political Thought of Jacob Burckhardt, John Stuart Mill and Alexis de Tocqueville*, Transaction, New Brunswick.

—2007, "Aristocracy in Tocqueville/De l'aristocratie chez Tocqueville," *The Tocqueville Review*, March.

Keslassy, E., 2000, *Le libéralisme de Tocqueville à l'épreuve du pauperisme*, L'Harmattan, Paris.

Ledeen, M.A., 2001, *Tocqueville on American Character: Why Tocqueville's Brilliant Exploration of the American Spirit is as Vital and Important Today as It Was Nearly Two Hundred Years Ago*, St. Martin's, New York.

Lévy, B.-H., 2006, *American Vertigo: Travelling America in the Footsteps of Tocqueville*, Random House, New York.

Lezard, N., 2004, *The Guardian*, April 3.

Mancini, M.J., 2008, "Too Many Tocquevilles: The Fable of Tocqueville's American Reception," *Journal of the History of Ideas*, vol. 69, no. 2, 245–68.

Mélonio, F., 1998, *Tocqueville and the French*, trans. B.G. Raps, University of Virginia, Charlottesville, originally published as *Tocqueville et les Français*, Aubier, Paris.

Mill, J.S., 2008, *On Liberty*, ed. Alan S. Kahan, Bedford St. Martin's, New York.

Montesquieu, Charles de, 1989, *The Spirit of the Laws*, trans. Anne M. Cohler, Basia Carolyn Miller and Harold Samuel Stone, Cambridge University, Cambridge.

—2010, *Pensées*, trans. Henry C. Clark, Liberty Fund, Indianapolis.

Pascal, Blaise, 2006, *Pensées*, http://www.gutenberg.org/etext/18269

Pierson, G.W., 1996, *Tocqueville in America*, John Hopkins, Baltimore.

Putnam, Robert D., 2001, *Bowling Alone: The Collapse and Revival of American Community*, Simon & Schuster, New York.

Riesman, David, 1965, *The Lonely Crowd: A Study of the American Character*, Yale, New Haven.

Rousseau, J.-J., 2009, *Discourse on Political Economy and the Social Contract*, trans. Christopher Betts, Oxford University, Oxford.

Sainte-Beuve, C.A., 1862, *Causeries du lundi*, vol. 15, Garnier Frères, Paris.

Schleifer, J.T., 1996, "How Many Democracies?," in *Liberty, Equality, Democracy*, ed. E. Nolla, New York University, New York, 193–206.

—2000, *The Making of Tocqueville's Democracy in America*, Liberty Fund, Indianapolis.

Schlüter, G., 1996, "Democratic Literature: Tocqueville's Poetological Reflections and Dreams," in *Liberty, Equality, Democracy*, ed. E. Nolla, New York University, New York, 153–64.

Tocqueville, A de, 1954, *Correspondance anglaise*, vol. 6, pt. 1, Œuvres complétes, ed. J.P. Mayer, Gallimard, Paris.

—1958, *Voyages en Angleterre, Irlande, Suisse et Algérie*, vol. 5, pt. 2, Œuvres complètes, ed. A. Jardin, Gallimard, Paris.

—1959, *Correspondance d'Alexis de Tocqueville et d'Arthur de Gobineau*, vol. 9, pt. 1, Œuvres complètes, ed. A. Jardin, Gallimard, Paris.

—1962, *Écrits et discours politiques*, vol. 3, Œuvres complètes, ed. A. Jardin, Gallimard, Paris.

—1967a, *Correspondance d'Alexis de Tocqueville et de Gustave de Beaumont*, vol. 8, pt. 1, Œuvres complètes, ed. A. Jardin, Gallimard, Paris.

—1967b, *Correspondance d'Alexis de Tocqueville et de Gustave de Beaumont*, vol. 8, pt. 2, Œuvres complètes, ed. A. Jardin, Gallimard, Paris.

—1967c, *Correspondance d'Alexis de Tocqueville et de Gustave de Beaumont*, vol. 8, pt. 3, Œuvres complètes, ed. A. Jardin, Gallimard, Paris.

—1970, *Correspondance d'Alexis de Tocqueville avec P.-P. Royer Collard et avec J.-J. Ampère*, vol. 11, Œuvres complètes, ed. A. Jardin, Gallimard, Paris.

—1977a, *Correspondance d'Alexis de Tocqueville et de Louis de Kergorlay*, vol. 13, pt. 1, Œuvres complètes, ed. A. Jardin, Gallimard, Paris.

—1977b, *Correspondance d'Alexis de Tocqueville et de Louis de Kergorlay*, vol. 13, pt. 2, Œuvres complètes, ed. A. Jardin, Gallimard, Paris.

—1983, *Correspondance d'Alexis de Tocqueville et de Francisque de Corcelle, Correspondance d'Alexis de Tocqueville et de Madame Swetchine*, vol. 15, pt. 2, Œuvres complètes, ed. P. Gibert, Gallimard, Paris.

—1985, *Selected Letters on Politics and Society*, ed. R. Boesche, trans. J. Toupin, R. Boesche, University of California, Berkeley.

—1987, *Recollections*, ed. J.P. Mayer and A.P. Kerr, trans. George Lawrence, Transaction, New Brunswick.

—1997, "Memoir on Pauperism," trans. S. Drescher, *www.civitas.org.uk/pdf/Tocqueville_rr2.pd*.

—1998a, *The Old Regime and the Revolution*, vol. 1, trans. A.S. Kahan, University of Chicago, Chicago.

—1998b, *Correspondance familial*, vol. 14, Œuvres complètes, ed. A. Jardin, Gallimard, Paris.

—2001a, *Writings on Empire and Slavery*, ed. J. Pitts, Johns Hopkins, Baltimore.

—2001b, *The Old Regime and the Revolution*, vol. 2, trans. A.S. Kahan, University of Chicago, Chicago.

—2002, *The Tocqueville Reader,* ed. O. Zunz and A. Kahan, Blackwell, Oxford.

—2003, "Speech on Socialism/The Right to Work," in *Alexis de Tocqueville and the Second Republic, 1848–1852: A Study in Political Practice and Principles,* ed. S.B. Watkins, University Press of America, Lanham, MD, 580–85.

—2004a, *Democracy in America,* trans. A. Goldhammer, Library of America, New York.

—2004b, Correspondence & Conversations of Alexis de Tocqueville with Nassau William Senior from 1834 to 1859, vol. 2, www.gutenberg.org/etext/13333.

—2005, "Second Memoir on Pauperism," http://dx.doi.org/doi:10.1522/24850019.

Watkins, S.B., 2003, *Alexis de Tocqueville and the Second Republic, 1848–1852: A Study in Political Practice and Principles,* University Press of America, Lanham, MD.

Zunz, O., 2006, "Tocqueville and the Americans: Democracy in America as read in Nineteenth-Century America," in *The Cambridge Companion to Tocqueville,* ed. C.B. Welch, Cambridge University Press, Cambridge, 359–96.

Annotated Bibliography

Tocqueville's Works in French

It seems that all Tocqueville's works will never be available in one place. Until the late twentieth century, scholars were compelled to makes use of Gustave de Beaumont's 1866 edition of Tocqueville, because it contained writings not yet published in the twentieth-century *Œuvres complètes,* published by Gallimard, which were begun in 1951 and still remained unfinished in 2013. Meanwhile, the *Pléiade* edition of Tocqueville and the new Gallimard *Lettres choisies* have overtaken the *Œuvres complètes* and include better-edited text with more notes and variants, as well as some letters not included in the *OC.* Finally, the Eduardo Nolla edition of *De la démocratie en Amérique,* by including, interleaved with the text, variants, notes and other documents, sheds new light on that work.

De la démocratie en Amérique. Edited by Eduardo Nolla. Paris: J. Vrin, 1990.
Lettres choisies, Souvenirs. Paris: Gallimard, 2003.
Œuvres complètes. 18 vols. Paris: Gallimard, 1951– .
Œuvres complètes. 9 vols. Edited by Gustave de Beaumont. Paris: Michel Lévy frères, 1864–66.
Oeuvres. 3 vols. Paris: Gallimard, Bibliothèque de la Pléiade, 1991–2004.

Tocqueville's Works in English

The recent wave of new translations of Tocqueville has left the reader of *Democracy in America* and *The Old Regime* (at least of volume one of *The Old Regime*) with considerable choice.

Two translations of *Democracy* need to be noticed because of their very different emphases. The Mansfield/Winthrop translation sets out to be a literal rendition of Tocqueville's French, obeying self-imposed rules such as always translating word "x" in French byword "y" in English. The Goldhammer translation, on the other hand, attempts a more traditional and more elegant rendering. Both, in their different ways, are superior to previous efforts. James Schleifer's excellent translation of the Nolla edition is now available in both bilingual and English-only editions from Liberty Fund. Of the new translations of *The Old Regime*, despite its undoubted flaws I prefer my own, which also includes an introduction by François Furet and Françoise Mélonio. The Kahan translation is also still the only one available for the bulk of volume two of *The Old Regime*, Tocqueville's notes and drafts for his projected continuation of that work.

Democracy in America. Translated by Arthur Goldhammer. New York: Library of America, 2004.

Democracy in America. Translated by Harvey C. Mansfield and Delba Winthrop. Chicago: University of Chicago Press, 2000.

Democracy in America. Translated by Gerald Bevan. New York: Penguin, 2003.

Democracy in America. Edited by Eduardo Nolla, translated by James T. Schleifer. Indianapolis: Liberty Fund, 2010 (bilingual), 2012 (English only).

The Old Regime and the Revolution. 2 vols. Introduction by François Furet and Françoise Mélonio, translated by Alan S. Kahan. Chicago: University of Chicago Press, 1998 and 2001.

The Ancient Regime and the French Revolution, translated by Gerald Bevan. New York: Penguin, 2008.

English-language sources for Tocqueville's other works are given here. In the last twenty years many of his writings have appeared in English for the first time, testimony to the upsurge in Tocqueville studies. Of particular note is the appearance of Pitts' translation of Tocqueville's writings on Algeria and slavery, and the recent publication of Tocqueville's post-*Democracy* correspondence with Americans and other post-*Democracy* writing concerning America by Craiutu and Jennings. The Boesche collection of letters and the Zunz and Kahan *Tocqueville Reader* also include some newly translated material. On the other hand, no new translation of the *Recollections* has appeared since 1970.

Alexis de Tocqueville's Journey to Ireland. Edited and translated by Emmet J. Larkin. Washington, D.C.: Catholic University of America Press, 1990.

Correspondence and Conversations of Alexis de Tocqueville with Nassau William Senior. 2 vols. Edited by M.C.M. Simpson. London: Henry S. King, 1872.

The European Revolution and Correspondence with Gobineau. Edited and translated by John Lukacs. New York: Doubleday, 1959. The "European Revolution" section is a translation of a portion of vol. 2 of *The Old Regime.*

Journeys to England and Ireland. Edited by J.-P. Mayer, translated by George Lawrence. London: Faber & Faber; and New Haven: Yale University Press, 1958.

Memoir on Pauperism. Edited and translated by Seymour Drescher. London: IEA, 1997.

"Political and Social Condition of France in 1789," *London and Westminster Review*, 3 and 25 (1836).

Recollections. Translated by George W. Lawrence. New York: Doubleday, 1970.

Selected Letters on Politics and Society. Edited by Roger Boesche. Berkeley: University of California Press, 1986.

Tocqueville on America after 1840: Letters and Other Writings. Edited and translated by Aurelian Craiutu and Jeremy Jennings. New York: Cambridge University Press, 2009.

The Tocqueville Reader: A Life in Letters and Politics. Edited by Olivier Zunz and Alan S. Kahan. London: Blackwell, 2002.

The Two Tocquevilles, Father and Son: Alexis and Hervé de Tocqueville on the Coming of the French Revolution. Edited and translated by R.R. Palmer. Princeton: Princeton University Press, 1987. This contains some excerpts from volume two of *The Old Regime.*

Writings on Empire and Slavery. Edited and translated by Jennifer Pitts. Baltimore: Johns Hopkins University Press, 2001.

Tocqueville's Life

The definitive biography of Tocqueville, that is, a work that gives
an adequate account of his life and times as well as his thought,
remains unwritten. The best single biography remains that of
André Jardin, first published in 1984. It suffers, however, from
lack of access to some materials now available, and from an
approach that was already dated at the time of publication. The
recent Brogan biography, while up to date in every respect and
charmingly written, is a poor introduction to Tocqueville's ideas.
On shorter periods of Tocqueville's life, Watkins' account of his
activity during the Second Republic (1848–51) and Pierson's
classic 1938 account of his trip to America provide all the information the reader might want.

Brogan, Hugh. *Alexis de Tocqueville: Prophet of Democracy in the Age of Revo-
    lution* (note the subtitle varies depending on the edition). London:
    Profile Books, 2006.
Jardin, André. *Tocqueville: A Biography*. New York: Farrar: Strauss and
    Giroux, 1988 (French edition 1984).
Pierson, George W. *Tocqueville and Beaumont in America*. New York:
    Oxford University Press, 1938.
Watkins, Sharon. *Alexis de Tocqueville and the Second Republic, 1848–1852:
    A Study in Political Practice and Principles*. Lanham, MD: University
    Press of America, 2003.

Bibliographies

There is an enormous and rapidly increasing secondary literature on Tocqueville. The reader can benefit from several bibli-
ographies that do their best to keep up with it. The online
bibliography maintained by Corcos is, inevitably, not 100%
complete, but is nevertheless an irreplaceable resource. The
annotated bibliography by Jardin/Mélonio is still useful, especially for its remarks on older works. The bibliography in the
Nolla edition of the *Democracy* is also very helpful.

Corcos, Christine Alice. "Alexis de Tocqueville, A Comprehensive Bibliography," http://faculty.law.lsu.edu/ccorcos/resume/tocque-bib.htm.

Jardin, André, and Mélonio, Françoise. "Bibliographie sélective et commentée," in *Alexis de Tocqueville. Zur Politik in der Demokratie.* Edited by M. Hereth and J. Höffken. Baden-Baden: Nomos, 1981.

Tocqueville's Ideas (Secondary Sources)

The works listed in this section are some of the most important and useful of the secondary literature on Tocqueville. Of particular interest and importance, beyond the Tocqueville Bicentenary issues mentioned here, is the *Tocqueville Review/La Revue Tocqueville.* Every issue of this biannual journal contains articles on Tocqueville as well as on Franco-American relations and other issues examined from a Tocquevillian perspective.

While many of the works here discuss *Democracy in America*, several are devoted solely to it. Schleifer's work is central to understanding of how the book was written. Along with Schleifer's book and the articles by him contained in the *Tocqueville Review* and other collections, the works by Lamberti and Drescher are at the heart of the debate over whether *Democracy* should be treated as one book or two quite different books. The collections of articles on *Democracy*, edited by Masugi and Eisenstadt, also contain many valuable essays.

Two other topics in Tocqueville's thought have attracted particular attention recently: religion and social reform. Goldstein's book is still the best treatment of Tocqueville's personal religious views. The article in Masugi by Hancock and Antoine's recent book give special attention to the role of religion in Tocqueville's thought, a topic that also enters into many of the general treatments of Tocqueville listed here. Tocqueville's thought on social issues and poverty has been largely neglected since Drescher's forays into this area in the 1960s. Now Drolet and Kesslasy have returned to the theme.

Antoine, Agnès. *L'impensé de la démocratie: Tocqueville, la citoyenneté et la religion.* Paris: Fayard, 2003. One of the rare studies to treat Tocqueville primarily as a political philosopher.

Audier, Serge. *Tocqueville retrouvé: Genèse et enjeux du renouveau tocquevillien français.* Paris: Vrin, 2004. An account of Tocqueville's place in contemporary French intellectual and political culture.

Benoît, Jean-Louis. *Tocqueville: Un destin paradoxal.* Paris: Bayard, 2005.

Boesche, Roger. *The Strange Liberalism of Alexis de Tocqueville.* Ithaca, NY: Cornell University Press, 1987.

Craiutu, Aurelian. "Tocqueville and the Political Thought of the French Doctrinaires," *History of Political Thought,* vol. 20, no. 3, Fall 1999, 456–93.

Drescher, Seymour. *Tocqueville and England,* Cambridge, Mass.: Harvard University Press, 1964.

—"Tocqueville's Two Democracies," *Journal of the History of Ideas,* vol. 25, 1964, 201–16. The original "two Tocquevilles" argument.

—*Dilemmas of Democracy: Tocqueville and Modernization.* Pittsburgh: University of Pittsburgh Press, 1968.

Drolet, Michael. *Tocqueville, Democracy, and Social Reform.* London: Palgrave, 2003. A look at a neglected area of Tocqueville's thought.

Eisenstadt, Abraham, ed., *Reconsidering Tocqueville's "Democracy in America."* New Brunswick: Rutgers University Press, 1988.

Furet, François. *Interpreting the French Revolution.* Translated by. E. Forster. Cambridge: Cambridge University Press, 1981. Not directly about Tocqueville, but contains a very valuable chapter about him, and a useful lesson in how Tocqueville has influenced contemporary historiography of the French Revolution, still dominated by Furet in the early twenty-first century.

Gannett, Jr., Robert T. *Tocqueville Unveiled: The Historian and His Sources for The Old Regime and the Revolution.* Chicago: University of Chicago Press, 2003. The definitive study on the subject.

Goldstein, Doris S. *Trial of Faith: Religion and Politics in Tocqueville's Thought.* New York: Elsevier, 1985. One of the best works on this vexed question.

Guellec, Laurence. *Tocqueville et les langages de la démocratie.* Paris: Honoré Champion, 2004.

Jaume, Lucien. *Tocqueville: les sources aristocratiques de la liberté.* Paris: Fayard, 2008. Particularly strong on the contemporary influences on Tocqueville, and also advances an interpretation of his work.

Kahan, Alan S. "Tocqueville's Two Revolutions." *Journal of the History of Ideas,* vol. 46, no. 4, 1985, 585–96. Argues that Tocqueville's projected volume two of *The Old Regime* would have emphasized class struggle.

—*Aristocratic Liberalism: The Social and Political Thought of Jacob Burckhardt, John Stuart Mill and Alexis de Tocqueville.* New York: Oxford University Press, 1992, reprinted with a new afterword in New Brunswick: Transaction, 2001. Sets Tocqueville's ideas in the context of a certain form of European liberalism.

Kelly, George Armstrong. *The Humane Comedy: Constant, Tocqueville, and French Liberalism.* Cambridge: Cambridge University Press, 1992. One of the rare works that puts Tocqueville into a comparative context.

Kesslasy, Eric. *Le Libéralisme de Tocqueville à l'épreuve de paupérisme.* Paris: L'Harmattan, 2000. An attempt, not very successful, to make Tocqueville into a proponent of a "third way" between socialism and capitalism.

Lamberti, Jean-Claude. *Tocqueville and the Two Democracies.* Translated by Arthur Goldhammer. Cambridge, Mass.: Harvard University Press, 1989. One of the strongest arguments for the "two Tocquevilles" thesis that alleges that *Democracy* should be treated as two books.

Lawler, Peter A. *The Restless Mind: Alexis de Tocqueville on the Origin and Perpetuation of Human Liberty.* Lanham, MD: Rowman & Littlefield, 1993. A Straussian interpretation of Tocqueville.

Lively, Jack. *The Social and Political Thought of Alexis de Tocqueville,* Oxford: Clarendon Press, 1965. Still an excellent introduction to his thought.

Locke, Jill, and Botting, Eileen Hunt, eds. *Feminist Interpretations of Alexis de Tocqueville.* University Park, PA: Penn State University Press, 2008.

Mancini, Matthew J. *Alexis de Tocqueville and American Intellectuals: From His Times to Ours.* Lanham, MD: Rowman & Littlefield, 2006.

—"Too Many Tocquevilles: The Fable of Tocqueville's American Reception." *Journal of the History of Ideas,* vol. 69, no. 2, April 2008, 245-68.

Manent, Pierre. *Tocqueville and the Nature of Democracy.* Translated by John Waggoner. Lanham, MD: Rowman & Littlefield, 1996.

Masugi, Ken, ed. *Interpreting Tocqueville's Democracy in America.* Lanham, MD: Rowman & Littlefield, 1993.

Mélonio, Françoise. *Tocqueville and the French.* Translated by Beth G. Raps. Charlottesville, VA: University of Virginia Press, 1998, originally published as *Tocqueville et les Français,* Paris: Aubier, 1993. The French version is much to be preferred.

Nolla, Eduardo, ed. *Liberty, Equality, Democracy.* New York: NYU Press, 1992.

Richter, Melvin. "Comparative Political Analysis in Montesquieu and Tocqueville." *Comparative Politics,* vol. 1, no. 2, 1969, 129–60.

—"The Uses of Theory: Tocqueville's Adaptation of Montesquieu," in Melvin Richter, ed., *Essays in Theory and History: An Approach to the*

Social Sciences. Cambridge, MA: Harvard University Press, 1970, 90–101.

Schleifer, James T. *The Making of Tocqueville's Democracy in America*. Chapel Hill: University of North Carolina Press, 1980. The definitive study of the subject.

Shiner, Larry E.. *The Secret Mirror: Literary Form and History in Tocqueville's Recollections*. Ithaca, NY: Cornell University Press. 1988. An excellent analysis of the *Recollections*, and especially of what Tocqueville didn't say.

The Tocqueville Review. In particular two special, book-length editions published in honor of the Tocqueville bicentennial celebrations of 2005: Vol. 26, no.1, 2005, which consists of a collection of the most important articles on Tocqueville published in the review since its founding in 1977, and vol. 27, no. 1, 2006, a collection of papers of unusually high quality given at some of the 2005 Tocqueville conferences.

Welch, Cheryl, ed. *De Tocqueville*. Oxford: Oxford University Press, 2001. A good introduction to *Democracy in America*, less so to *The Old Regime*.

—*The Cambridge Companion to Tocqueville*. Cambridge: Cambridge University Press, 2006.

Wolin, Sheldon S. *Tocqueville Between Two Worlds: The Making of a Political and Theoretical Life*. Princeton: Princeton University Press, 2003. Despite its many flaws, still interesting.

Zetterbaum, Marvin. *Tocqueville and the Problem of Democracy*. Stanford: Stanford University Press, 1967.

Index